Harmony for the Heart

Devotionals for Young Women

Elaine Berry, Author & Compiler

Each devotional is identified by the writer's key signature. The
key signatures are coded to the author's names on pages 204-207

Green Pastures Press

Harmony for the Heart

ISBN 1-884377-08-4

Green Pastures Press
HC 67, Box 91-A
Mifflin, PA 17058

We dedicate this book to our parents:

> *Roger and Anna Lee Berry*
> *Elvin and Doris Eberly*
> *Duane and Sharon Eby*
> *Eli and Verda Glick*
> *David and Ruth Glick*
> *Hubert and Mary Graybill*
> *Mark and Esther Kuepfer*
> *Michael and Vanita Martin*
> *Vernon and Kim Martin*
> *Harold Dean and Ruth Miller*
> *Vernon and Leona Troyer*

Thank you for the wisdom and love you have shown. God bless you for the investment you have made in our lives.

Special thanks to Roger and Anna Lee Berry, Harold Dean and Ruth Miller for their help in reviewing the manuscript.

Preface

Long, metal wind chimes clang in the storm's aftermath. Dainty white chimes tinkle in the early morning breeze. Wind produces the beautiful sounds. Harmony comes when the chimes sway and knock against each other.

We all want our lives to produce a harmonious sound. We don't like the winds of trial, the hard knocks that we get in life. We want our lives to be calm and still. But, like the wind chimes, true beauty is not produced until we are moved. The sound that comes when the wind blows against us is what God is looking for.

God has been moving in our lives. Sometimes it brings pain, sometimes joy. Sometimes we wonder why we face the struggles we do. Then we see the big picture and the lovely music God is producing.

That's what we've written about in this book. In sharing the things God is taking us through, our prayer is that you will be encouraged. Whether you're sixteen (and wondering what the future holds) or thirty (and still single), our prayer is that the harmony of God's love will fill your heart.

Elaine Berry

Contents

That we should be
to the praise of His glory . . .

   . . . Singing and making melody in your heart to
the Lord;
   Giving thanks always for all things unto God and
the Father in the name of our Lord Jesus Christ.
                      Ephesians 1:12; 5:19, 20

Chapter 1

God Is So Good

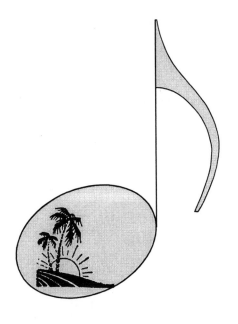

What Jesus Means to Girls

READ: Psalm 23

Jesus, You are my Shepherd—
You lead me where green pastures grow.
        The most loving Shepherd.
Jesus, You are my Brother—
You love me and forgive my wrong.
        The most forgiving Brother.
Jesus, You are my Doctor—
You care for me when I am sick.
        The most caring Doctor.
Jesus, You are my Creator—
You made me in a special way.
        The most ingenious Creator.
Jesus, You are my Savior—
You gave your life to set me free.
        The most gracious Savior.

Jesus, You have satisfied me.
You've supplied everything I need.
        You're all to me and I love you!

All Charges Are Cleared

READ: Romans 5:6-21

Sometimes stress can come in the form of a little yellow envelope with the words "OFFICIAL NOTIFICATION ENCLOSED" written in red letters.

Not another notice, I groaned as I tore open the envelope in frustration. My stomach knotted as I absorbed the attack on my character. "...Our good faith effort to allow you this privilege has been faulted by your lack of appropriate action in this matter."

But I did act! I had indeed paid for the items I received from this company. Now they were sending another bill for items they told me I had received; but in reality, I had not. I had even written them a letter explaining that.

My spirit wilted as I continued to read: "It would certainly be acceptable that your failure to pay...were based on a real problem. However, your failure to notify us of such occurrence implies that this is not the case."

I tried to calm myself before I reached for the phone to call the company's credit manager. This had been going on far too long.

I explained the predicament as nicely as I could to a very helpful gentleman. What joy pulsed through me as I heard his words come singing over the phone, "All charges are cleared!"

Debt-free. Not beholden anymore. I could throw the envelope away.

I remember the ecstatic feeling I experienced when I realized my debts—the ones I really did owe—were paid in full. When I realized it was *my* sins Jesus paid for when He died on the cross.

Paid in full! All the charges cleared! My account was settled long ago. Jesus' blood sends a message stamped in bright, red, unfading colors: "I HAVE PAID THE PRICE. SHE IS FORGIVEN. NO ONE CAN CHARGE HER ANYMORE. THIS CHILD IS MINE."

It's a message that reaches across time. It's for you and me. It's for ALL people. It will give us a refuge when we stand before the Great Judge. It gives us a passport to heaven.

It'll be joy when I can worship in His presence for eternity.

Thank You, Lord!

Hill of Praise

READ: Psalm 113:1-6

"Look how beautiful the sunset is!" exclaimed my friend as she paused in her ascent up the hill.

I looked, but wasn't impressed. I was at a lower elevation than she was, and decided that apparently she saw something that I didn't.

When I reached that height, I, too, was awed by the splendor. None of it had been evident at the bottom of the hill. The rest of the neighborhood went about their business, unaware of what we were witnessing. Trees obscured their view of the beautiful sunset.

Sometimes you may feel like life is boring: the world goes on day after day, always the same old thing. Or maybe life is full of sadness, deaths, tragedies, or natural disasters, and you don't see the purpose in it. Everything seems to go wrong.

How can you rise up out of the valley of despondency and see the beauty of life? By climbing the hill of praise. Praise God for who He is and for what He has done. Remember His promises. Thank Him for your blessings, for all the good things in life. Sing and smile.

As you climb the hill of praise, more and more of the glories will be revealed. Once you reach the top, you will be amazed at how bright the outlook is.

Reaching the top of one small hill of praise doesn't necessarily mean that you will see all the beauty and understand all the meaning of life. There will always be more heights to climb and more to see and experience. One glorious day you will enjoy the perfect beauty of heaven with no recollection of the sadness below.

Christmas Year-round

READ: John 1:1-15

We were all enjoying our week of summer Bible school, but nothing was that different from other years. We were used to the routine of classes, lessons, singing, and everything that accompanied Bible school, and knew what to expect. That is, until one particular evening.

We had returned from our classes, and the song leader was taking selections from the children. A flaxen-haired, blue-eyed girl raised her hand.

"Yes, Laura," the song leader said, "What would you like to sing?"

"Silent Night," she replied.

Smothered laughter rippled through the audience. A Christmas song in the middle of summer! Yet, as I looked into that innocent face, so sweetly singing of Jesus' birth, I was deeply impressed. She was unashamedly honoring her King. He was *real* to her.

Swallowing the tears, I realized that she had grasped something that I had not. Christ was not merely a Bible character celebrated at Christmas time. Christ was my Savior, and His birth changed the destiny of my life! His redemption is available all the time. Is it not only right to honor Him the whole year long?

It Takes a Drought

READ: Hosea 10:9-13

ain!

It takes a month without rain to fully appreciate it. I hear the wonderful sound washing the dust from the roof. The scorched blades of grass lift their heads and revive. After a day with temperatures over 100 degrees, cool rain makes Missouri feel like a place fit to live in once again.

God!

It takes a dry season in my life to truly appreciate Him. I feel His presence bringing a soft peace to my soul. My sin-burnt heart reaches out to God. My parched spirit soaks up the presence of the Father, making life feel worth living once again.

That's when I wonder, *Would God mean much to me if there were no dry times, times when He seems distant or even unkind?*

Over and over, God has shown me His answer: It takes a drought.

Lord, Thank You!

READ: Psalm 100

Lord, thank You that You're always there,
Ready to help me; ready to care;
Ready my heaviest burdens to bear.

Thank You for knowing what each day holds,
Help me to count my blessings untold,
For You've given me mercies past silver and
gold!

The last couple of times that we've had prayer meeting I've classified the prayer requests "Praise" or "Request." This is what I came up with three of the times that I did it.

PRAISE	REQUEST
33%	67%
11%	89%
0%	100%

This might not be an overall average, but indicates that the amount of thanks is rather low. How is it in my everyday life? Is it better or worse than at prayer meeting?

Lately, I have been trying to be more thankful, for several reasons. First, because the Lord deserves it. Secondly, it makes life look better when I am counting my blessings instead of my trials. It's easier to accept my lot in life and make the best of it. Thirdly, if I count my blessings I will be more enjoyable to be with and make it easier for others to count their blessings.

As I grow older and encounter more trials I want to learn to give thanks at all times. I hope you do too!

Don't Go With Them

READ: 2 Chronicles 20:20-26

That day was probably the worst day of the whole Bible school term. A mild stomach flu had been going around, and I felt like it was trying to land on me. The classes didn't sink in, and I felt like doing some serious grumbling.

Then, I remembered a chapel message about thanksgiving we had one morning. I smiled, said something to God, and went on with my classes. My stomach felt a little less queasy, and I was able to concentrate again.

What had I done? I simply told God, "Thank You, God, for these things that are happening to me. I praise You because You are trying to do something in my life."

I'll never forget that chapel message I heard at Bible school. It changed my whole outlook on life. Now, when bad things happen, I remember some quotes from that message.

"When I praise God for everything, I change on the inside."

"Praise is the deepest commitment we can make. It gives heaven the authority to act on our behalf."

"Grumbling is sin."

"One of the best ways to rob the devil is to praise God."

"When things go wrong, don't go with them."

I praised God for that lesson on thankfulness. After I started praising God for everything, it was hard to stop.

Then, I realized that I felt happy even when everything in my day seemed to go wrong. When Satan brought temptation to try to distract me, I told God, "Thank You because You are going to use this temptation to make me a stronger person.

That's just what God did. Now, when things go wrong, I try to praise God instead of going with them.

With the Price of the Passage

The cheese was molding; the bread was getting stale. In the hold of the ship, the family was restless. It would be weeks until the shoreline of America would be in sight.

At last the father dipped his hand into his pocket and brought out a coin. He handed it to his oldest son and said, "I'm tired of all this complaining about the food. Go above deck and see if you can find some fruit or fish to buy."

The son was gone a long time and the family began to wonder where he was. Perhaps he was lost or had gotten into trouble. Another hour passed. Then two. At last, the father decided to see if he could locate his son.

His search led him to the door of a large dining hall. The tables were loaded with all kinds of attractive food. Sitting at one of the tables was his son, eating as if the food was free!

"Son, how can you do this?" the father pounced upon him as the boy was stuffing his mouth with cake. "You know I cannot afford to have you eat this way!" He hauled his son off the chair, spilling a basket of white rolls with his elbow.

"But wait, Dad!" the boy quickly swallowed his mouthful and smiled at his father. "This meal—as well as all meals served here—is included in the price of the passage."

I love that little story! What a puny life of discouragement I sometimes live, sitting in the dark hold of a ship nibbling on moldy cheese and stale bread. I sit in my dark little circle of misery, trying to satisfy my hunger by the pleasures of the world.

I don't realize there is a luscious feast that God has spread for me in His Word. "He brought me to the banqueting house, and his banner over me was love" (*Song of Solomon 2:4*). It is free dining ready for me to enjoy—included with the price of the passage.

21

Rejoicing in Him

READ: Luke 1:46-55

"Did you bring mail for me?" I asked eagerly.

"No, there is none for you," was the reply.

No mail! My heart sank. But someone had developed my film. Excitedly I opened the envelope, only to be devastated because none of the pictures were mine. My pictures must have been in someone else's envelope. "What a rotten day," I moaned inwardly.

Later that night as I tossed and turned in bed, my mind raced with negative, depressing thoughts. No letters. Not one!

Then a gentle voice interrupted my thoughts. "Last week you got lots of letters. Why are you complaining now?"

I ignored that rebuke. What about my pictures? If I didn't get letters, at least I could have seen my pictures. Again I heard that quiet voice. "The negatives in the envelope are yours even though the pictures weren't. Next week someone can take the negatives to develop."

I wallowed in self-pity and didn't want to change my attitude. Then I thought of the verses from Habbakkuk 3:17-19. Habbakkuk said that even if the crops failed and the animals died, he would still rejoice in the Lord. That stopped my complaints.

It's so hard to rejoice in the disappointments and frustrations of life. It's hard to count the blessings when the troubles seem insurmountable. But I am commanded to rejoice. Many times it is difficult to thank God for the situation, but I thank Him for being in control and acknowledge that what He is doing is for my good. I rejoice because God is still there for me.

Chapter 2

Search Me, Oh God

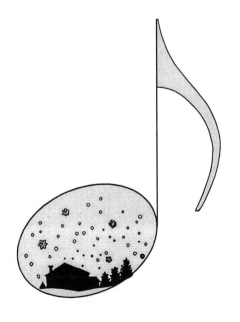

Monday Morning Laundry

READ: Ezekiel 36:25-27

<u>7:30 a.m.</u>

In the laundry, I pile grimy shirts into a wash basket. Smelly socks land on the corner pile. What a lot of dirty wash!

Lord, are you in the laundry business today? I'm bringing You my spirit. All last week I dragged its smells with me: pitying myself, lapsing into pride, and venting my displeasure on others. But You've opened my eyes, Lord. I can't endure this revolting ugliness another minute.

Pile towels into the washing machine. Drizzle soap over the load. Pull the switch to start the washer churning. Plunge a stained shirt into a bucket of sudsy water.

O Lord, forgive me! And please cleanse my spirit. Will You wash it in Your righteousness? Scrub away the pride and selfishness. Rinse my spirit in Your grace, that I may be clean and white through You.

<u>3:00 p.m.</u>

My hot iron presses the wrinkles from cotton dresses. I arrange the crispness on wire hangers.

My spirit needs pressing too, Lord. Press it into Your own. Make it as pure and loving as Yours.

I stack sweet-smelling towels on bathroom shelves, and hang fresh dresses on closet rods. Now we'll have clean clothing for one more week.

I don my laundered spirit. (It feels so much better! Why

did I clutch its filthiness?) Your grace, Lord, is so fresh and free that I can sing again. And I'm sure that You'll keep me supplied all week, even if the potatoes burn, my brothers are noisy, and it rains every day. Thank You, Lord!

You Can Do Better

READ: 1 Corinthians 9:24-27

I lowered my red pen to mark another answer wrong. Helplessly, I shook my head as I looked at my student's test. "This is ridiculous!" I exclaimed to the now-empty classroom.

Beside the grade, I printed these words: *You can do better.*

I knew that my bright and talented student was capable of more than a seventy-eight percent. I knew she hadn't done her best. I shook my head again. *This has got to stop,* I determined. *She's never made grades like this before. She's not even trying.*

The lack of effort in my student frustrated me. As a teacher, I had done my part. I provided what she needed in order to do well on the test. I reviewed the facts, and was there to help if she didn't understand a difficult concept. But, if she didn't try to do her best, what was the use?

Then, I realized that I, too, had done poorly on several tests that had come my way recently. I had been irritable when my students had a hard time understanding a simple concept. New truths in the Bible weren't there, because I didn't feel like digging for them. Prayer time had become a real drudgery because I didn't put myself into it completely. I was wrapped up in myself, but thinking more of others took too much effort. Little things that I knew I should give up were carefully reserved for myself.

Discouragement threatened to settle in when I realized that something wasn't quite right in my life. I didn't like the feeling of guilt that stalked me, but I didn't feel like putting forth the effort that a thorough surrender required.

The Holy Spirit convicted me with the same words I had written on my student's test: "You can do better. You can spend more time in prayer and fasting. You can be more sensitive to those around you. You can seek for more opportunities to tell others about Me. You can dig into my Word a lot deeper. You can work on becoming more and more like Me and being more patient with your students."

God has done His part. He's provided everything I need to know. He's there to help me in my difficulties. But if I don't try, what's the use?

I know I can do better.

A Bath Please

READ: Psalm 51:1-10

"Me bath," my two-year-old sister begs.

"Wait," we often say. "It's not time for a bath." Sometimes it's the middle of the morning. At other times it is necessary to finish putting away wash.

She is sad when we tell her to wait; but when we say, "Come, let's go," she is excited and happy again.

Sometimes, like my little sister, I need time to cleanse and refresh my soul. Maybe I didn't spend much time in prayer that morning. Or maybe I am feeling proud because last night I said just the right thing to a sister at church.

So, I'm feeling empty, and my soul is pleading, "A bath please!" But, I'm too busy. It's 10:30 in the morning, schoolwork must be done, or I need to change the wash and sweep the floor. Well, sorry, God, there just isn't time.

I rush to get my work done, and the foreboding feeling remains in my heart. Maybe I manage to push most of it to the back of my mind, but then my little brother does something to annoy me. He gets a tongue lashing because I'm not at peace with myself. The experience leaves me with a dirtier heart, a hurt brother, and a Savior waiting for me to come to Him.

It's not hard to take a spiritual bath. Here are four of the main steps:

1. Prepare myself. (Step into some private place where I am not likely to be found and where there are no interruptions.)

2. Step into the shower. (Get down on my knees.)

3. Turn on the shower. (Start praying, telling the Lord how I feel, asking Him to give me His peace. Then, my

Heavenly Father, who is waiting with His abundant store, will shower His blessings over my life. Refreshing. Cleansing. Renewing.)

4. Scrub. (Just like I have to scrub harder if I'm really dirty, sometimes I have to pray for a while till I feel a change and cleansing.)

I should never be too busy to take time for a soul bath. Instead, I may need to take one several times a day. That will help me to live a strong, joyful Christian life until Jesus returns. I want to go take a shower right now!

Recording

READ: Job 16:19; Romans 14:10-13

Mattresses from cribs in the nursery room are the perfect things to reduce floor noises in the church. The chorus director and recording engineer situate the mikes on them. We are ready to begin our day's work.

The first few songs are fun. Practice the song first. Then, record. Everyone hums the pitch. Complete silence. The recorder clicks. Watch the director. All together on the first word. Finish the song. Hold our breaths until we hear another click. Sit on the benches or risers to listen to what we just recorded. Grab a drink or snack on grapes and watermelon.

Then comes the debate. Was that song good enough? Shall we go over it again? Invariably, someone says, "What will we lose by recording it again?" Everyone scurries to their spot, clearing their throats for the final time. We repeat the song.

Eight hours later our voices are hoarse. Some have headaches. My contact lenses are dry. The words we're singing match my feelings: "I am tired, I am weak, I am worn..."

I come home and plop down on the couch. "Whew!" I say. "Never again will I criticize another chorus's tape."

What makes me say that? I have been there. I know how exhausting recordings can be. When I hear a mistake on a tape, I will picture the work that went into that song. In doing that, I'll overlook the faults.

Perhaps there are other people I wouldn't criticize if I saw the whole picture. The girl I think is grouchy and snobbish may be going through struggles that I know nothing about. The boy that tries to act tough might really be insecure. I would probably understand my parents' rules better if I could look at life from their viewpoint.

Whether I like it or not, God is recording every unkind word and uncharitable thought. There won't be any retakes on my life. What's it going to sound like?

Prayer of Repentance

READ: Psalm 32

"I wanted to witness, but somehow my tongue was tied. My testimony didn't match my actions. She left with that hungry, soul-sick look in her eyes, and I shed bitter tears. What happened to that once-joyous life in You?

"I've wasted so much time being foolish and self-centered. Often I have sensed somebody's hurt, but ignored it because I didn't know how to relate. I covered up my own insecurities and hurts by being bold and trying to have "fun." Still, I was grieved that I could not meet the spiritual needs of my peers.

"I longed to do something great for You, and I failed to see that Your work for me was here at home. I lost sight of You, and became harassed with daily cares. I was impatient with my siblings, swamped with the workload, and frustrated with our busy schedule. I did not ask You for relief, I told myself that You did not care.

"I have broken many vows, and violated Your laws. I implored You to give me answers, but You were silent. In times of suffering, You seemed far away. I realized then that I brought trials on myself because I could not let go. I ranted incessantly, trying to accomplish my goals, not realizing that all along You were working things out in Your perfect plan and timing.

"I'm sorry God, for failing You so completely. I see now that You truly care and I ask You to transform my life. To Your most holy will, oh God, I now gladly resign."

Tortillas, Worry, and Wonder

READ: Proverbs 21:2-4

"Please don't watch me," I begged my Belizean friend. "This is my first time, and I feel really clumsy."

Teasingly, she bent over the table and studied the tortillas I was trying to make. Suddenly, my fingers felt thick and bulky.

If my friend hadn't been watching me so close, I could have made a nicer tortilla. I had watched her pat out tortillas earlier that day. Her fingers had moved across that ball of dough as rapidly as an expert typist's hands move across a keyboard. Next to her tortillas, mine would have looked like-like-well, like a beginner's tortillas. Which is *exactly* what mine were!

It's not just in making tortillas that I'm scared by people who can do it better than I can. I'm scared to speak Spanish around people that speak it well. I can't expect to know Spanish as well as people that have been to language school or have grown up speaking it. Why, then, do I feel so embarrassed about my beginner's Spanish?

People that are more experienced writers frighten me too. Beside their glowing stories and heart-touching articles, my manuscripts look flat and lifeless. I think, *Why not just let all the people that can write so much better than I do all the writing?* I tremble at seeing my name in print, because I'm sure someone will think that there are a lot of other people who could do better.

What is it in me that's scared of misshapen tortillas, broken Spanish, and poorly written articles? I could call it a lot of things. I could name it "fear of failure." That has a nice,

31

pathetic sound to it. I could also call it "low self-esteem." That sounds even better.

Know what God calls it? He talks about it in James 4:6: "God resisteth the proud, but giveth grace unto the humble."

Pride. That sounds bad. Now that I think about it, though, I can trace a lot of the fears in my life back to pride. I realize how much of my life I have wasted in worrying about my performance, worrying about what other people think, worrying about how I look.

God's telling me I need to replace the worry with wonder. He wants me to wonder how pliable my heart looks to him rather than worrying how my tortillas look. I should be wondering what God thinks of the words I say instead of worrying about my Spanish. God wants me to wonder if my writing is bringing glory to Him, rather than worrying about what people will think of the writer.

Lord, thanks for using a tortilla to remind me of how I look to You.

A Clean Backyard

READD: Colossians 3

I tended to keep my front yard clean: the mowing, the raking, the weeding, the trimming—those obvious things in my life that other people saw first. I made sure I was kind and considerate. I held my temper because the Bible says, "Let not the sun go down upon your wrath." I tried to be a cheerful giver and worked at surrendering my life completely to God.

But in my efforts to keep my front yard beautiful and weed-free, I had let the back yard grow up in ugly thistles. When I opened my back door to look, the view appalled me. There was an "inordinate affection" (Colossians 3:5) in my life, big ugly thorns of fleshly desires.

I fell to my knees, tears dripping off my cheeks, as I began to pull the ugly weeds. "Dear God, deliver me from the influence of myself."

And God reminded me:

"He that trusteth in his own heart is a fool: but whoso walketh wisely, he shall be delivered" (Proverbs 28:26).

"For if a man think himself to be something, when he is nothing, he deceiveth himself" (Galatians 6:3).

"But God forbid that I should glory, save in the cross of our Lord Jesus Christ, by whom the world is crucified unto me, and I unto the world" (Galatians 6:14).

Today, at times, my greatest fear is that I will again get too busy in the front yard and allow the back yard to grow up. Never in the Christian life can I put my gear in neutral.

It's a continual struggle, a continual growth, a continual swimming against the tide, and I'm glad I'm not alone in it. The Holy Spirit will be there to prompt me. My brothers and sisters in the Lord will be there to remind me, checking up on me when I am too close to see myself in perspective.

Take a tour of your back yard. Maybe you—like me— hadn't been there for a while. Maybe you haven't been there for so long that you forget what it originally looked like in its pristine beauty of freshly cleaned, blood-washed pureness.

Thank God you won't have to clean it alone.

When God Sends Frost

READ: Proverbs 3:11,12; Hebrews 12:5-8

Were you ever overly contented with yourself? Did you ever tour your heart's garden, then strut after latching the gate? I have.

You'll find your exultation to be like late summer. Wait a little. When the pink impatiens burst with bloom and the marigolds glow golden, frost falls.

I remember particularly one month last winter. Having settled myself nicely into age seventeen, I took inventory of my life and smiled smugly. I thought I'd finally arrived. Three separate incidents within one month shattered that attitude.

A cunning temptation parked itself at my feet. I reached. Thank God for the friend sent to stop me! I shuddered that night when I realized what might have happened. Wasn't I a little above falling?

Mom and I went to the mall together. I was shopping for clothing, but we couldn't agree on what was appropriate. After pouting, I was shocked, Hadn't I yet conquered that rebellion?

Our family was traveling home from Pennsylvania over snowy roads, and I was driving. What began as confusion climaxed four seconds later as an accident. I rolled our van, with everyone in it. I was horrified.

Several weeks passed before I realized what God was doing. He was showing me what I really was. It was humbling. Embarrassing. But definitely worthwhile.

It was as if frost had come. Gone were all pretenses and self-made righteousness, just as frost leaves impatiens with only slimy leaves.

After showing me my worthlessness, God reminded me of His power. He can use a worthless person best! The thought brought a peace as gentle as new snow on a frosted landscape.

Have you noticed frosted flowers in your life? Perhaps God has a message for you also. Then, with me, you can praise Him for those experiences.

> Thank You, God of the seasons,
>   the frost, and
>   the snow.
> *You* know
> when we begin to trust ourselves;
> and then You keep us humble,
> down where You can use us.

The Great Physician

The operating room was cold. I shivered as I lay on the narrow table. Bright lights glared in my face, and gowned figures moved soundlessly about the room

What am I doing here? I thought. Panic rose within me. *These doctors are going to cut into my head! Can I trust them?* However, I couldn't back out now. I was totally in their hands.

"Relax," my mother whispered, squeezing my hand reassuringly. I smiled faintly. Yes, I knew that this surgery was my only hope if I wanted to hear again. Jesus would help me through this. Breathing a prayer, I fell asleep.

* * *

Slowly, my mind came through the fog. A doctor was bending over me, watching me carefully. Oh, the excruciating pain that seared my head and neck! How could I bear this?

A month passed. I found myself back at Johns Hopkins Hospital, nervously waiting. Today my implant would be activated. What if a cochlear implant wouldn't work for me?

"I love you, Rosina," I heard my dad say.

What? Voices! I could *hear* them!

Pain was forgotten. Fear was tossed out the door. My world became alive once more!

* * *

The Great Physician is often operating on our lives. Many times we writhe on the uncomfortably narrow table. Begging God to let us alone, we refuse to take the bitter medicine he has prescribed for us. We push away the stinging needle that injects the Holy Spirit's power into us.

We are afraid of the sharpness, the bitterness of God's work.

Relax. God knows what he is doing. He is working for our ultimate good, and watches over us carefully.

The pain will pass. When the Great Physician has finished his work, new life will be awarded to us. We will live in the warmth of His presence. What joy!

What's Taking Away My Appetite?

READ: Ephesians 4:17-29

"My son has fever, diarrhea, and stomach pain. I think he has parasites," his mother stated.

Some Guatemalans think that parasites are the root to a lot of their health problems. Sometimes that is the case.

Parasites are organisms that live off another living thing. They don't contribute anything. Instead they take advantage of their host. A few examples of parasites in humans are lice, ticks, worms, and amoebas.

Parasites rob people of good health and take away their appetite. Some parasites eventually destroy a person if they aren't treated.

Sins are like parasites. They rob me of my joy and peace,

take away my spiritual appetite, and cause leanness of my soul. They ruin me spiritually if not confessed.

Maybe the parasite of jealousy is eating away at my insides. Do I compare myself with my friends? Am I envious because they are married, or live in a nicer house or have a new car?

Am I harboring the parasite of anger or bitterness? The more it is fed, the bigger it gets. I can only hide it for a while, but sooner or later it will become obvious and will result in a lot of pain.

Some parasites make me proud of my accomplishments and my own righteousness. Others make me think only of myself and my rights. Parasites cause relationship problems. They feed on juicy gossip and pass it on to others. The list could go on.

What should I do if I have parasites? Comb my life daily to check for them. Confess them to God and ask for His cleansing. He is the Great Physician who prescribes the right medicine to remove the parasites. He's on call twenty-four hours a day and is waiting eagerly to rid me of them. I also need to feed on the vitamins of God's Word to replace the nutrients I've lost. At times it is a slow process, but I will not let the parasites win.

Betrayed by My Speech

READ: Matthew 26:68-75

"You were talking to someone from Ohio, weren't you?" my brother asked after I finished my telephone conversation.

"How did you know who it was?" I asked.

"I didn't," he replied. "But you talked with a northern accent.

I have a tendency to copy the accent of the people I'm with. That ability is helpful in learning a new language, but it can be annoying when people say, "I know who you've been with lately. You talk just like her."

Jesus' disciples had a distinct accent. People knew because of how Peter talked that he had been with Jesus. Peter denied Jesus three times, but he could not escape the truth. His speech betrayed him.

I've been thinking about that lately. If people can tell whom I've been with by how I talk, can they tell when I've spent time with Jesus and when I haven't?

Lord, I haven't been around You enough lately. I'm not talking like You. I'm sorry for all those attitudes and words that came out when I didn't spend enough time with You. Please forgive me, and help my speech to betray that I've been with you.

A Snow White Heart

I looked out my bedroom window one morning in astonishment. During the night, the sky had showered its fluffy treasures all over the ground. Now, I could only see a beautiful, white expanse of snow.

But while the snow awed me with its beauty, it also reminded me of tragedies that had happened during cold winters. Two girls that I knew had been killed because of the snow and ice. I thought of how much their families must miss them, and of how quickly the same thing could happen to me.

I wondered just how ready I was to meet my Maker. Was my heart as pure as the sparkling snow on the ground? I remembered saying some not-so-good things about people. I thought about attitudes I had that I really wouldn't want to take with me into death. I asked God to help me be willing to get rid of those things in my life.

The good thing is that God can forgive me and make my heart as clean as the snow, if I just ask Him. I realize that if I become a stronger Christian because of the deaths of those young women, they will not have died in vain. Just as the snow melts and spring bursts into bloom, I too can have a snow white heart that is growing with new life.

Chapter 3

I Surrender All

Strength in Weakness

READURE: 1 Corinthians 1:23-31

Run a few miles. Drop on the floor and do pushups. Lift weights and watch those muscles bulge.

Strength. Health. Fitness. Energy. I enjoy physical exertion in work or recreation. I like to keep myself in shape.

Yet my primary quest for strength is of an entirely different nature. This kind of strength I cannot obtain by mere effort and determination. In fact, the only way I can acquire this strength is through weakness.

The clay will only mold when it is soft. The wheat cannot make bread until it is crushed. The alabaster box will pour forth fragrance when it is broken. God can use me to carry out His purposes—when I am soft, crushed, and broken.

Strength lies in placing all my ideals, desires and ambitions on the altar, and offering them to God. Then, stripped and weak, I kneel before the altar, and ask for His will. His strength is manifested in my weakness.

Paul said in 2 Corinthians 12:10, "When I am weak, then am I strong." No, strength is not obtained by human endeavor. It is found in weakness.

My Favorite Place in the World

READ: Matthew 16:24,25; Galatians 2:20

My favorite place in the world is not an earthly location. Rather, it is a condition of my heart reached by dying to self. It's a place of COMPLETE SURRENDER. What peace, what joy, what blessing, and what fulfillment this place brings! When I dwell there, no one, no event, no circumstance upsets me or takes away my peace. As long as I maintain COMPLETE SURRENDER in my heart, my response to difficulties is Christ-like. As soon as I leave this place, perfect peace also leaves, and my responses become flesh-like.

The dictionary says that surrender means "to yield to the power of another or relinquish possession of; to abandon." This is exactly what Jesus called me to when He invited me to be His disciple. He longs to see me relinquish the power and possessions of my life and what I call "my rights." Every step of discipleship calls me to surrender.

COMPLETE SURRENDER confronts me most in everyday living. I have found that to pray as Christ asks, I must surrender other activities, such as late night reading (which I dearly love) or lazily lying in bed in the morning. Sometimes I'm tempted to justify myself if some other member of the family doesn't get up early. COMPLETE SURRENDER calls me to obey the words of this song: "Though none go with me, still I will follow."

Another aspect of family life that calls for COMPLETE SURRENDER is giving up activities I want to do to let others have time for what they want to finish. COMPLETE SURRENDER also calls for a soft answer when I think others have taken advantage of me in one way or another.

I realize that COMPLETE SURRENDER is not just for the big decisions in life. Rather, I need to be willing to abandon everything for Jesus' sake, whether big or small. If I surrender to the Lord, I will receive His full blessing upon my life.

When Fudge Is a Failure

READ: Romans 7:15-25

It was one of "those" days.

I was making my traditional fudge for Father's Day, and things weren't going right. First, I discovered that I needed a twelve-ounce can of evaporated milk, but I had already used half of the last can in a dessert that was in the oven. A cookbook said to substitute three-quarters cup milk and three tablespoons margarine for light cream. So I broke the rule I thought I had taught myself: *Never substitute!*

The stuff didn't thicken like it should have. I knew I couldn't go on boiling it forever, so I added the chocolate chips, A minute later I discovered there was something wrong *there*. The chocolate chips weren't melting! I poured the thin concoction into pans. The stuff looked more like vomit than fudge.

If the success of my life depended on how I made fudge, my life would be a failure, I thought. I smiled, then sobered.

Of course I would not measure my life by the success of my fudge making. But what were other expectations, other standards, that I—or society around me—had set up for myself?

What happens when my ideal meets the real?

Sometimes life just plain doesn't go the way I thought it would. Sometimes my dreams become nightmares. Sometimes other people let me down. Sometimes I let myself down.

Like my fudge, life can get a little messy sometimes.

Did I set my scopes too high? Or maybe, was I following the wrong ideal? Was it the standards of men over the principles of God? My will or God's will?

Like Lot's wife, I tend to look back and follow natural desires to see what the world is doing. Instead, I must keep my vision clearly focused on God's country ahead.

It's a daily battle of, "Who's on the throne?" The old nature says, "How do I fit God into my plans? How can I get God to give me what I want? How can I get God to change that person?"

The new nature, driven with power by the resurrected Lord has a different attitude: "How do I fit into God's plans? How can I get myself to give in to what God wants? How can I allow God to change me?"

With sights set on sanctified things I can rejoice because "...Sin shall not have dominion over you: for ye are not under the law, but under grace" (Romans 6:14). I need to brush off the dust, recharge my heart with Divine strength, and keep on going.

And yes, when the next Father's Day rolls around, I will make fudge for my dad.

Freedom

READ: John 8:31-36; Galatians 5:1

Freedom! With a shout of exhilaration, I shot down the hill on my sled. Clouds of snow showered me as I flew through the dazzling whiteness. The wind whipped my red cheeks and frosty hair. I yelled again from sheer pleasure. Sailing down that snow-covered hill, I felt so free!

Freedom. How I have wished that I could tear down the bars that withhold my freedom! Surely I could be truly happy if I could escape the prison of restrictions. If only I could evade pain, the merciless ripping of my bleeding heart. If only I could be free from loneliness, sinful temptations, and dominating selfishness, free from the bitter consequences of my sin.

Struggling relationships, grappling with God, questions that demand answers...authority, rules, tears. Why can I not be free from all of that?

The secret of true freedom slowly unfolds. Almost against my will, I begin to see that all my life I have actually been fighting freedom.

Freedom lies in a total surrender of my will to God, an unconditional obedience to His plan, and joy in His work. Submitting to authority, admitting my wrong, and giving abundantly of myself pave the road to freedom. When I am totally honest with God and with other people, I find liberation.

Yet, in a land fairer than this, I will find the height of freedom. My struggles, pain, fears, and suffering here will enhance the transcendent freedom in heaven. When I gaze at the face of Jesus, I will know true freedom. For if the Son will make me free, I shall be free indeed.

46

As Far as Possible

READ: 1 Thessalonians 5:21-24

"Make sure you don't get your fingers caught," Mom warned me as we stood before our old wringer washing machine.

I shivered at the thought of my finger going between the rollers and coming out smashed.

Why, then, did I try to see just how close my fingers could come to the rollers before they went through? I was a child at the time, and there was something inside me that wanted to see how close to danger I could go.

Yesterday, I saw some children outside playing the same game. A pile of leaves was burning, and the children tried to see how close they could get to the fire without getting burned.

Haven't young people outgrown that game? I'm afraid not. I've played it before. I've seen others play it, too.

• Young people…
  who see how often they can skip their Bible
  study and prayer and still be a good Christian.
• Teenagers…
  who want to find out just how wild their
  music can get before their parents confiscate
  the tape or CD.

I heard a story once about a king. He wanted to find a coach driver to safely drive the prince and princess to the castle at the top of the mountain. The road was narrow, and the king wanted a skillful driver.

Many people applied for the coveted position. Each one was asked, "How close can you get to the edge of the road without tumbling down the mountain?"

"A few feet," one man boasted.

"Inches," another man bragged.

Only one man gave this answer, "Why, sir, if it were the king's children, I would want to stay as far from the edge as possible."

Guess who got the job.

The King's children are too precious to risk an overturned carriage. The King's children are too valuable to see how close they can get to danger.

If the King's children want to reach the beautiful castle, they need to stay as far away from the edge as possible.

Walls

READ: Ephesians 2:13-17

In this complex human society, we are constantly building walls around ourselves. These walls are built to protect, to shelter ourselves from outside interference. As we busily, perhaps unconsciously, build these walls, we fail to realize the devastating consequences.

There are the gates of communication. Within our homes and communities, thoughts and phrases float around.

"I don't feel like talking, so I'll just ignore her."

"I'm afraid he won't understand how I feel. I won't even try to explain."

"They don't care what I do. I'm not going to bother asking them about it."

"I don't know how to relate to her in this situation. I'll just leave her alone."

"He's shy. He'd rather not go with us anyway.'

"I can have a lot of fun with her, but I just can't get close to her."

There are the mental posts.

"I'm okay the way I am."

"Someone else can take that responsibility."

"He's crippled. He'd spoil our game."

"Dad and Mom are so old-fashioned! They don't understand this age!"

"I'm too busy to help out with that need. I'm not educated or experienced enough either."

"No one could have a way much better than mine."

There are the concrete spiritual blocks.

"God never *specifically* said I couldn't do it."

"I'm so tired tonight, I'll just skip reading my Bible."

"Well, God knows what I want and how I feel, so I don't really need to pray."

"Oh no, God would never make me do something I don't want to do!"

"What the minister preached doesn't apply to my situation."

"I don't have to give *everything* up. As long as my heart is right, the rest doesn't matter."

Yes, the walls of self-protection are rising. Every day, more gates, posts, and blocks are laid. Still, there is a rallying cry to fling open the gates, knock out the posts, and crush the blocks to rubble.

Break down the walls! If they remain unbroken, they will bar us out from the kingdom of heaven.

I Wasn't Scared!

READ: 1 Peter 5:5; Ephesians 6:2,3

Our front door is lower than the street level, so we have to go up steps to leave the house. One day while my grandparents were visiting, my grandpa started up the steps ahead of us. At the top he lost his balance and fell about three feet to the concrete below. Thankfully, he only had some bruises and a cut or two on his fingers. But for those of us who saw him tumble, it gave us a real scare.

All of us, that is, but my ten-year-old brother. "I wasn't scared!" he commented later.

I told him, "That's because you are younger and don't realize like we do what could have happened."

As I pondered the incident and the difference between my brother and me, I thought, *Sometimes I'm just like he is. There are things I want to do, but my parents don't want me to. I say, "I'm not scared. I don't see anything wrong with it. I cannot see any reason why I could get hurt.*

But those who are older can see the dangers in light of experiences that I don't have. They have seen the results of falls that I haven't seen.

I want to listen to those who can see spiritual or physical dangers that I can't. There's protection in submission.

Chapter 4

Victory in Jesus

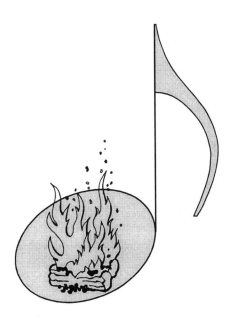

The Fires of God

READ: 1 Peter 1:3-9

"Oh, God, *must* it be so?" I cry out to God, time and time again. My flesh wants to cringe, to run away from it. In my human thinking, I feel like I would be a much better Christian if I would not have this struggle. I face it every day. I fight bitterness that wants to creep into my heart. It's the worst trial of my life.

"It's not fair!" I have told God. "Why? Why must I live with this? How can I face this?"

One night during revivals at Bible school, I discovered how wrong I was to question God. The evangelist preached on the fires of God. He told a story of how a man was watching a refiner of gold. The refiner kept adding heat, until finally, the onlooker asked him, "How long do you need to keep that fire burning?"

The refiner answered, "Until I can see my reflection in it."

What a beautiful picture of what God wants to do in my life! His ways are perfect. I see the discomfort of today; He sees the reflections of His image He is producing in me.

I also remember that evangelist's closing comment: "We are going to face the fires of God sometime. If we run away from it in this life, we will face it at the Judgment."

If I forget everything else I learned at Bible school, I'll never forget that the only way to face my problems is with Jesus by my side. Running away from the fire will only hinder me.

God has said, "My grace is sufficient for thee; for my strength is made perfect in weakness." It's a promise. God will give me the grace to endure the fire and experience a joyful, abundant life in Him!

After the Fire

READ: 1 Kings 19:9-12

It doesn't feel good to get burned. It feels even worse to be right in the middle of flames of adversity. Sometimes it feels like I might melt.

My journal portrays best the heat and smoke I was battling:

Oh, God, what shall I do? I don't believe I've ever reached a level of stress this high. My prayers have become nothing but one big word: "Help!" Why doesn't God give clearer direction? I've never prayed so desperately, but no answer comes. What am I lacking? Why am I so confused, frustrated, scared, and hurt? Why do I feel so alone? How much should I trust my feelings? A child of God should not feel this way! "Save me, O God; for the waters are come in unto my soul...I am weary of crying; my throat is dried: mine eyes fail while I wait for my God" (Psalm 69:1,3).

I was like a duck—calm on the surface, but paddling like mad underneath. And the water was hot!

But God's purposes are so different from ours. "If thou

faint in the day of adversity, thy strength is small" (Proverbs 24:10). He knew the limit to my strength; or rather, *I* knew that there was no limit to *His* strength.

After the fire comes a calm. The crackling is gone, the smoke has cleared.

God tenderly cleaned the soot off my heart with the clear water of His Word. Several journal entries later:

There's joy in the Lord! "When there is nothing left but God, we find that He is all we need."

Hold on to His joy!

That's a Fact

READ: Romans 4

My elbow bumped against the concrete floor as I situated myself on the narrow air mattress.

"I wanna wish you a Merry Christmas from the bottom of my heart," blared the music from the house beside the school. It was after midnight, and some of the villagers were celebrating the arrival of Christmas Day with firecrackers, music, and partying.

Christmas? Sleeping on the floor in a schoolroom didn't *feel* like Christmas. The day before hadn't *felt* like Christmas either. We had traveled from southern Belize to northern Belize. When we stopped to help a stranded motorist on the Southern Highway, the bus had become stifling. That wasn't the kind of day-before-Christmas weather I was used to.

As Christmas Day progressed, I still didn't *feel* like it was Christmas. I had never drunk coconut milk, eaten a chicken foot, or played volleyball outdoors on Christmas Day. I enjoyed every minute, but had to keep reminding myself that it really was Christmas.

Putting *feelings* before *fact* is one of my tendencies. If I don't *feel* like God is working everything together for good, it's hard for me to accept the *fact* of Romans 8:28. If I don't *feel* like someone has treated me fairly, I forget the *fact* that I need to love that person.

Sometimes, a bad day will affect my *feelings* and cloud the *fact* that God wants me to be joyful in spite of how I *feel*. Even if one of my contact lenses rips for no apparent reason or I stumble over rubbish the puppy drags onto the porch, I can't let my *feelings* dictate my life. If I did, I would kick the puppy and snap at everyone around me, forgetting the *fact* that I should give thanks in everything.

There's another *fact* that I used to have a hard time believing. The promise that God is able to keep us from falling was hard for me to grasp, because I *felt* like I could never have victory over my sinful nature. That's where *faith* had to come in. My brain had registered the *fact* that God could deliver me, but I could never experience complete deliverance until I accepted that *fact* by *faith*. When I wallowed in the *feeling* that my case was impossible, God couldn't get anywhere with me.

My *feelings* still get in the way sometimes. When they do, the quickest solution is to find a Bible verse that applies to the situation and hang on to it. My *feelings* may fluctuate, but I know God will always be there when I need deliverance. That's a *fact*!

I Can't...He Can

READ: Judges 6:11-16

"God, I can't do it. You're asking me to do something that's too difficult," I silently pled.

"Why can't life stay just as it is?" I complained. "I don't need any more responsibility or any more hassles. I've had enough changes in the past months to drive me crazy. Now I am being asked to take on more work in the clinic."

"Haven't you been praying that I would provide a remedy for the dilemma?" God's question pierced my soul. "This is my answer. Are you willing to sacrifice a little in order that your prayer will be answered? Or are you thinking only of yourself?"

I knew I needed to accept God's answer. I felt at peace about my decision, yet at the same time, I was scared about the future. I felt incapable of handling this new commitment. My morning prayers became pleas for God's help.

Some days were tough, but God gave me the strength that I needed for each day. As the weeks and months passed, I realized that I was gaining more confidence, and that I didn't dread each day so much. I began to actually enjoy my new responsibility. I rejoiced as I saw the way God was leading me and enabling me to carry on His work.

Why do I have a tendency to rely on my own strength instead of on God's? Life goes so much better when I trust Him for the strength I need each day. He never deserts me. May I always remember the lesson I learned from this experience—to put my confidence in God instead of in myself.

Climb Every Mountain

READ: Joshua 14:6-13

Climbing Squaw Peak was a real trial for me. My friends and I woke up at 4:30 a.m. just to make it to the top of the mountain before the sun got too hot. I dreaded the climb; if my friends hadn't been pushing me to go, I'm sure I never would have had the experience.

As we started out, the path wasn't too bad. Frequent stops to take a drink helped our wheezing lungs to rest. As the path became steeper, our bodies felt heavier. Sometimes we simply had to haul ourselves onto the rocks above us. After an hour of tiring work, we finally reached the top. We looked at the landscape far below us, and knew that everything had been worth it. We had made it!

That experience taught me to think "I can" instead of "there's no way I can do this." When a dreaded job or a difficult trial looms in front of me, I *can* overcome it. And just as my friends motivated me to climb Squaw Peak, God is my everlasting Helper in everything I face. He wants me to climb every mountain in my life, and to do it with His strength.

Roots

READ: Hosea 14:4-7

In our backyard we had an old orange tree. Because its bark was coming off, we decided to take it out. We didn't just want to cut down the tree and burn out the stump; we wanted to put a new tree in the same place. So, the boys dug around the roots. Every time they got to a root, they cut it. After they had dug down several feet, they tried pulling it out. They couldn't.

So they kept digging. Down, down, cutting roots, digging dirt. They tried again. The roots rocked, but did not come out. More digging, pulling. Each time after trying to pull it out, we dug some more, and found yet another root that was holding it fast. Finally, after many hours of digging, pushing, pulling, straining, and cutting, it came out.

What about me? What kind of root system do I have? Small and shallow? Thick five inch roots that go deep? Do I have roots of faith, patience, and love for God in my life?

I want my roots to grow so that I will be a healthy tree. Then, no matter how much Satan tries to dig and cut, my roots of faith in God will remain unmoved.

Focusing System

READ: Micah 7:7-9

ye exams can be a real pain sometimes. It's especially bad when they flip lenses in their machine, and ask if I can see better with number one or number two. After a while, I can't tell any difference between the two.

At my last eye exam, the optometrist flipped a lens and asked which lens I could see better with. "I don't know," I said. "It's hard to tell a difference."

The optometrist whistled. "She's got one whale of a focusing system," she said. "She focuses so fast that she can't tell a difference. That good focusing system makes up for a lot of other problems with her eyes."

I don't know much about eyes, other than that they are extremely complex. I have a feeling, though, that it would be terrible not to have a focus. I've looked at photos where the camera didn't focus properly. They're all blurred. I've heard of people who see double at times. That would be a scary experience. I'm thankful for my focused eyes even though I need high-powered contacts or glasses so that I can see.

I just wish that strong focusing system in my eyes would carry over into my spiritual life. It's tough to keep my focus on Jesus. Far too often, my spiritual vision blurs. Distractions come. I can't make rational decisions because everything looks fuzzy.

Jesus. Focus. Two words that can make a difference in my life. I don't have to blur my spiritual perception by trying to look at Jesus and myself at the same time. I turn to Him, allowing tears of repentance to clear my vision. I turn to Him, saying, "Jesus, help me to focus on You."

That helps with a lot of other problems in my life.

59

Who Touched Me?

READ: Luke 8:43-48

"Who touched me?" Questioningly His eyes swept the group around Him. Fishermen, tax collectors, Roman soldiers, and Pharisees were probably all there. Strange that He should notice anything unusual in that tight mass of people.

Who had touched Him? Instinctively, his eyes lighted on a head in the audience. No, it wasn't a fisherman or a banker. Neither was it a Pharisee. It wasn't a scowling Roman. It was a woman.

"Who touched Me?" Jesus asked again. Trembling, the lady pushed through the crowd. She threw herself at Jesus' feet and told Him her story. She had touched Him to be released from the terrible disease that had racked her body for years. Now she was frightened of the consequences of her daring act.

"Daughter," Jesus said gently. "Your faith has made you whole. Go in peace."

"May I touch Him?" As a young person, you may be facing soul-sickness. You wrestle with discouragement. You find it hard to stand alone when "everybody else does it." You really want to do what is right, but when you're with your peers, you get carried away. You agonizingly wonder if your unsaved friend can see Christ in your life.

Perhaps your circumstances are ideal. You may be surrounded with model Christians that seem to know exactly what to do and say. You may feel that your ideas (and even your relationship with God) fall far short of theirs. Thus you feel inferior, and afraid to approach God.

You might be disappointed in yourself. You have set high goals, and when you fail to reach them, you sink into a swamp of "*Why* did I do that?" or "*When* am I going to grow up?"

Likely you also go through the wilderness of loneliness. Perhaps you are deserted because of your moral standards. Or, maybe you live in a Christian environment, but haven't found that bosom friend you need. Sometimes you're surrounded with family and friends, yet you still feel dreadfully alone.

There is hope for you. Regardless of who you are, there is room for the trembling, scarred soul at the feet of Jesus.

To that sin-sick soul, there is healing. There is a light in the darkest valley. There is that Hand, reaching for you to lift you out of your troubles. There is life, hope, and love awaiting you.

He is here. You can touch Him. You will never be the same.

Focusing on Jesus

READ: Matthew 7:1-5; Hebrews 12:1,2

I was recently frustrated as I tried to help some fellow church members organize a special meal. It seemed like we weren't unified. Even though we all had the same goal, petty jealousies and misunder-standings hindered us. We became judgmental and critical of one another.

I struggled with my attitude toward others. When I was wondering how I could change that attitude, I realized that it depends on whom I focus.

For instance, if I was in a room with some friends, and a very important person like the Queen of England walked into the room, my attention would turn to her. I would no longer focus on my friend's outlandish dress or the overly talkative, annoying woman beside me. I would be more interested in what the Queen of England had to say and what I could learn from her.

Shouldn't it make a difference if Jesus is in my heart? When my focus is on Jesus, I won't criticize how my friends talk or act. In my desire to be more like Him, I will become more aware of the areas in my life in which I need to change, and less aware of the faults of others.

Chapter 5

Does Jesus Care?

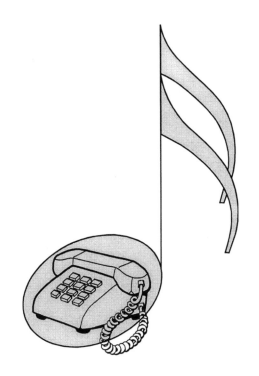

The Hand of the King

READS: *John 20:24-29*

Miserably,
I huddled in the darkness.
Frozen tears were sliding down my face.
My heart felt cold,
lonely,
and battered with pain,
extreme
relentless
pain.

I whispered in the darkness,
"Where is the King?"

He came.
He surrounded me with warmth.
He reached down
deeper
than
anyone
had
ever
gone,
and touched my heart
with a hand so gentle,
the old wounds opened up and bled profusely.
Then,
they could heal.

Smiling through my tears, with the dawn on my face,
I looked at that hand,
holding mine.
Suddenly,
I understood.
I looked at that hand,
the hand of the King,
and
it
was
scarred.

Leave Your Toys

READT: 2 Samuel 22

The baby sat on the floor, playing with a tiny toy. Grinning and cooing to himself, he seemed happy and content. Then, he spied it. A box lay at my feet with some papers in it. Fascinated, he scooted toward the box, his tiny hands reaching eagerly for the papers.

"No!" his mother told him.

The baby wanted those papers. He touched them. The mother picked him up and set him down some distance from the box.

"WAAAAAAA!" Heart-broken cries came from the baby's mouth. Tears rolled down his pudgy cheeks. His mother handed him another toy, but he didn't want that. He kept on sobbing.

Then, the mother reached out her hands. The baby grasped them, and hung on tightly. Soon he was in his mother's lap. A peaceful and secure look replaced the pout.

I smiled at his childishness. From a grown-up's vantage point, the papers were insignificant. In a few years, the baby would see that too.

Have you ever been like that baby?

An opportunity for service suddenly closes. A job you had wanted isn't available. A young man you had thought might be the one for you decides that you're not the one for him. Someone you thought was a friend turns her back on you. Your family moves to a place where you don't feel like you fit in. Everything you had planned in your life is totally rearranged.

You can sit on the floor and cry. That's OK. Disappointments hurt.

However, you don't need to stay sitting on the floor, pouting. There's a hand reaching out to you. Behind that hand is a loving Father, a Father who sees from a viewpoint that you don't understand.

This Father also cares. He knows you're hurting, and understands that it's a part of your developing process. He wants you to grow up, and He realizes that disappointments will help you to do that.

Reach out and take the hand God offers you. Leave your toys and find peace and security in the One who loves you more than anyone else ever will.

I Shall Rise

READ: Psalm 42

I am depressed. Depression hangs over me like a polluted cloud, stifling any bit of existence that longs to be pleasurable. It wraps me in its heavy shawl, hot and smothering.

I am depressed. Depression swallows me in a murky pool full of predators. The dank waters suck me down, laughing maniacally at my misfortune. I struggle to hold my head above the mire, but the waters sneer, blocking out the sun with their blackness. I sink, robbed of any ephemeral happiness in life.

I am depressed. Depression stares at me through the dark windowpanes. I see the stark skeletons of trees, the shadowy distance of the moon, the fragility of the night air. I see them as images of the thing I am, skeletal, cold, shattered.

I shall rise! Sunlight pushes away the dark clouds, and bathes me in warmth and gladness. My spirit breathes deeply, and takes wing. It flies high above the cloudy valley, and carries me on to the ecstasy of freedom.

I shall rise! God's gentle hand, with utmost tenderness, lifts me from the swamp. It sets me in the flowing streams, the streams of healing. Sparkling pure, the water washes all worldly filth from my marred soul. I find myself in lush green pastures, whole, clean, and alive. The waters of the joy of life have returned.

I shall rise! I look again through the windowpanes. I see the fluttering of a butterfly, the brilliance of the sun, the restoration of the invigorating air. I see them as expressions of the person I now am, suffused in freedom, radiance, and restoration.

Lost Parakeet!

READ: Luke 15:4-7

I'll let my parakeet, Payasito, write the devotional for me this time. I feel he could say it better than me.

"Hi, friends. I'll tell you something that happened to me about two weeks ago. My owner, Karen, opened the door of my cage and left the room. I said to myself, 'This is my opportunity to look around.'

"Anyway, I walked over to the living room. After looking around for a while, I gradually got to the kitchen and dining room. I was pecking at the wooden chairs, when I heard Karen holler out to her mom, 'Where's Payasito? Have you seen him around?'

"'No, I haven't seen him. Why?'

"'I had his door open, but I can't find him anywhere. I looked all over my room, but he's not there.' Karen sounded desperate. 'Maybe he got outside. I'll go look. Oh, I hope I can...' the words faded away as the door slammed shut.

"Hearing footsteps outside, I figured she was looking for me. The footsteps came nearer, and stopped outside the kitchen door.

"I guess she saw me right then, because she came running over to me. Tears filled her eyes as she picked me up, and cradled me close. 'Payasito, I was so worried about you.'

"After she told her mom about finding me, she took me to my cage and latched the door.

"As I thought over it in my bird brain later, I recalled the songs that Karen sang to me sometimes. I thought about one that told about a little black sheep that got out from the flock one day. Feeling really lonely, he thought that the shepherd probably wouldn't even miss him. Because he was a black sheep, he felt worthless. But then the shepherd's dog found him. Even though he had run away, the shepherd loved him. Even though I ran off, Karen still loved me and was happy to find me again."

Thanks, Payasito. Sometimes, we feel worthless, maybe because we're different from others or can't do something as well as others can. Or, we wish we'd be taller or shorter, and the list goes on and on. Maybe we have left the Shepherd like the sheep did, and don't think He even cares about us anymore. I'm so glad that even when I left Him sometimes, He always found me again and still loved me.

I have to think of the shepherd in the Bible. When he found the little lost lamb, he said to his neighbors, "Rejoice with me; for I have found my sheep which was lost."

Beyond Our Suffering

READ: Romans 8:17-21

Suffering. What a bitter cup! What is the purpose of so much inner pain, devastating experiences, and crushing trials?

We have all walked through dark valleys, often wondering why it must be so. We retreat behind false fronts, displaying cheerfulness and witticism. Inwardly, we are torn and bleeding. Because friends cannot fully share our suffering, our only hope is God. Sometimes even God seems cold and distant.

Then, we are compelled to lift our empty hands to Him, and allow our fainting hearts to trust in His goodness. He will hold our hand tightly all the way, and even carry us when we are too tired to move.

Suffering has a wonderful way of enhancing inner loveliness. Just as an alabaster box pours forth perfume when broken, if we are shattered into a thousand pieces, an indescribable sweetness will flow from our lives.

Yes, we know that the highest waters cannot drown out His love. In this silently hurting world, our suffering can be a channel to reach those who have no hope. For some of us, there is the light of the cross burning down the dark aisle, but some cannot see even that.

Consolation at Midnight

READ: Isaiah 53

My hidden heart that had been locked away,
was slowly, gently,
introduced to the light,
warmed and softened.
Now,
the door has slammed!
The wounds have been raked afresh,
and the bleeding heart
recedes
into silence again.
The pain is more than I can bear.

But,
surely, He has borne my grief
and carried my sorrows.
He was despised, rejected,
a man of sorrows,
and acquainted with grief.
He was wounded for my transgressions,
He was bruised for my iniquities,
and with His stripes, I am healed.

With His stripes,
I am healed.

Does God Hear?

READ: Psalm 91:14-16

Have you ever wondered, down deep in your heart, if God *really* hears you when you pray? I have!

One day, one of my friends and I went with two other ladies to visit a school several hours away. We badly wanted to be home that night in time for the youth Bible school meeting. We especially wanted to take in the women's class. Unfortunately, that happened to be scheduled first in the evening, and we were afraid we would miss it.

We started home late. As we calculated the time, we realized that at the rate our driver was going, we would probably miss the first part of the service. We fidgeted in that back seat! If there had been a way to push the gas pedal from where we were, we would've done it.

But God was teaching us an important lesson about trust. Over the tape player came the words, "Just a little talk with Jesus makes it right."

We looked at each other and whispered, "Let's pray!"

Even after we had prayed, my faith (if you could even call it that) was very small. Humanly thinking, there was hardly any reason that the class would not be over. However, God's thinking is not human thinking.

As we got out of the vehicle and looked into the church, we saw something. For some reason, the evening classes had been switched. In spite of all our worrying and fretting, God had worked it out that we could be there for the women's class.

That class was a double blessing. God had strengthened my weak, crumbling faith. Yes, He *had* heard us! He showed me that He cares about the smallest details of my life.

I don't need to wait for an experience like that, though, to remind me that Jesus hears. He promised over and over in His Word that He would. Isaiah 65:24 says, "And it shall come to pass that before they call, I will answer; and while they are yet speaking, I will hear."

But I have a part to play. I need to put all known sin out of my life and abide in Jesus. Then, He says, "Ask, and it shall be given unto you; seek, and ye shall find; knock, and it *shall* be opened unto you."

I thank God that He hears my heart's cry, and answers in His perfect will and time.

Every Little Detail

READ: Psalm 103:13,14; 1 Peter 5:7

ometimes I've thought that it takes special talent to drive a straight shift pickup, and I wasn't blessed with it. Besides lacking the talent, my feet barely reach the clutch.

One Wednesday night Mom and Dad were away. Since they had the car, I had to drive the truck to prayer meeting. My younger sister, her friend, and I piled into our rusty Ford.

We came to the divided highway. The truck stalled in the median. I turned the key. The motor died. I tried again, but my foot slipped off the clutch. I wasn't used to driving that truck with my Sunday shoes on, and they were slightly slick on the bottom.

"Pray, girls," I said as I reached down to turn the key again.

I let up on the clutch while pushing down on the gas pedal. A few jerks, and we were breezing down the highway.

About two hours later, we sat in the truck again. "Let's pray that I'll make it home without stalling," I suggested. We all bowed our heads in silent prayer.

Guess what? The truck didn't stall once on the way home. I'm beginning to think driving that truck doesn't take special talent, just prayer! I'm amazed that God cares about little details like that. He understands my frustration when that gear shift doesn't want to slide into second gear. He cares when I stall the truck, and He's there to help.

There are other day-to-day frustrations He cares about too.

He understands how I feel when I've just hung out the wash and it starts raining. He cares about my agitation when I'm sewing and I have to pick out the same seam four times. He sympathizes with me when I'm tired and face a counter full of dirty dishes. He's there to help me stay sweet in the middle of a hectic day if I ask Him.

He knows how I feel when I'm trying to teach my students something, and they don't understand it. He knows the impatience I feel with students when they fail to follow directions, or when they stumble over reading simple words. He's there to help me stay calm when I feel like pulling out my hair.

He cares when I miss my family or when it seems like no one really understands me. He knows how I feel when I have tough decisions to make. He's there to comfort and guide me if I ask Him.

Thank You, God, for caring about every little detail of my life.

Leave a Message After the Beep

READ: 2 Chronicles 7:14,15; Philippians 4:6,7

"Hi, you've reached the Jones residence. Sorry we can't come to the phone right now, but leave a message and we'll get back to you. Maybe."

When I heard a message similar to this one day, I had to applaud those people for being honest, if nothing else. They made it obvious that they would call me back when they wanted to, and only *if* they wanted to.

Have you ever played phone tag with someone—you know, when you're both trying to get in touch with each other, but keep missing? Or were you ever on the phone for ten minutes listening to an automated message telling you what number to push next? If you have, I'm sure you know the frustration of not being able to communicate properly.

Something that always encourages me in these situations is the thought of that one place you can call twenty-four hours a day, seven days a week, and always get in touch with the Person you need to talk to. And, regardless of what part of the world you're calling from, the number is toll-free! You know the place—God's house.

Isn't our Lord great to have made a way for us to talk with Him any time? His method is much better than cellular phones; beepers; and, definitely, answering machines. Imagine how it would feel to call on God and get a recording that says, "Leave a message after the beep. If I feel like getting back to you, I might." I'm thankful we don't have to deal with that!

Let's take time out of our busy days, call on God, and

thank Him for the tremendous privilege of being able to speak with the Creator of the universe. He will always answer the call.

Quadratic Equations

READ: 2 Chronicles 14:10-13

I slammed my math book shut in defeat. Those quadratic equations and graphs were simply impossible to do. Didn't Mr. Overholt realize that I would never understand, despite all his patient explanations? Besides, what good would quadratic equations do me in five years from now?

Suddenly it seemed that God was speaking to me, "Kathryn, how about asking Me to help you? Why don't you try Me, and see if I can't help you understand?"

So I humbly bowed my head and asked my Heavenly Father for help. The next time we had math class, I was amazed! Things began to make sense in my mind. God had answered my cry for help.

"Lord, help me to learn a lesson from this experience. Help me to realize that You not only help with the big problems, but You even want to help me with little things like quadratic equations."

Chapter 6

Let the Beauty
of Jesus be
Seen in Me

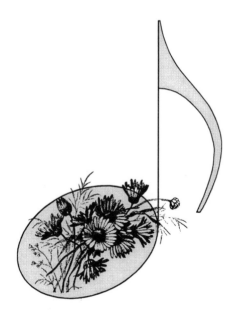

Under the Light

READ: John 15:4-8

At a youth retreat recently, one of the girls did a chalk drawing for us. Under a regular light we saw one picture, but under a black light, the first picture faded and a second one appeared.

At the same retreat we heard a message on being holy because Jesus is holy. That made me think about how Jesus wants the world to see His life in me.

My life is like the chalk drawing. When people look at me, the first thing they see is my human body. However, when God's light is focused on me, it does what a black light does to a chalk drawing. It draws out the hidden picture, Jesus living in me.

So that others may always see the glorious reflection of Jesus in me, I must stay under His light at all times. As soon as I try to shine on my own, the image of Jesus disappears and they can only see carnal me once more.

Oh that I would truly learn what it means to abide continually in Jesus, and in that way *always* reflect God's glory.

A Chapter on Beauty

READ: Ruth 2:1-12

Although my waistline measures 25 inches, and I weigh 110 pounds; if I have not God's gentleness, I am not beautiful.

And though my complexion is clear, and though I have no pimples, and though my skin is smooth and tanned; if I have not God's grace, I am not beautiful.

And though my hair is neither frizzy nor greasy, and though it parts only where I want it to part; yet if I have not God's kindness, I am not beautiful.

God's beauty doesn't depend upon my appearance, for it is beauty of spirit. It is gentleness and patience. It thinks first of others; it lets a friend interrupt. God's beauty sings while it presses dresses, and smiles at the crippled neighbor. It stretches a warm touch to a hurting sister. God's beauty listens to an overwhelmed friend.

God's beauty can't be purchased. I can't buy it by the yard from a bolt of lace; neither can a store sell it in a powder can or tube of lipstick.

God's beauty never grows old. But glossy hair will turn gray and fall out. A slim waistline will grow flabby, just as pink cheeks will fade.

But God's beauty can shine on a wrinkled face and live in the clasp of a trembling hand. It can still sparkle from faded eyes.

When I was ignorant, I tried to be beautiful by myself. But, when I understood God's ways, I realized that only God's spirit within me can make me beautiful.

And I may have charm, form, and beauty, these three. But the greatest of these is God's beauty.

True Ugliness

READ: Proverbs 6:34, 35; Song of Solomon 8:6

My great-great-grandfather was ugly. In fact, he was so ugly that he entered a contest for the ugliest man in Madison County. The prize was a six-dollar pocketknife. In those days, that was quite something. John Berry wanted to win that prize.

He didn't. Another man, whose last name was also Berry, won the pocketknife. Poor great-great-grandfather John came in second. Furious, he vowed never to speak to the contest winner again.

Years later, my father rode the school bus with a boy named Tommy Berry. Tommy was a descendant of the contest winner. "Don't you play with that boy," Dad's parents told him. "Those people aren't fit to be with."

My great-great-grandfather's jealousy had affected the generations after him.

Thankfully, I don't have to deal with that family feud. I've risen above my mountaineer ancestors. Or have I?

I don't envy people who are ugly, but I do have a problem with envying girls who are pretty. (After all, I am a descendant of the second-to-ugliest man in Madison County!) Why do some girls have perfect complexions and beautiful noses, and I don't?

On top of envying girls that are pretty, sometimes I'm jealous of girls that know exactly what to say and do to make everyone like them. Deep down inside, I'm envious when I see people flocking around a certain girl.

No, I can't honestly say I never struggle with jealousy. Even though it's different than what my great-great-grandfather faced, it's still ugly. It can still ruin relationships, infest good attitudes, and hack at my spiritual life.

Jealousy is the opposite of contentment. It's what the Bible calls covetousness. And covetousness is—well, it's sin. It's in the list of sins in Mark 7, along with murder and all those other horrible sins. Now that's true ugliness!

Lord, erase this ugliness from my heart. Take away those envious desires. Replace them with a willingness to put other girls first, even if they are prettier or more popular than I am.

Beautiful?

READ: 1 Peter 3:3-6

rack!"

Pain shot through my head. I crumpled to the ground.

"Rosina!" my sister shouted. "Are you hurt badly?"

"I-I think I'll be okay soon," I stammered, still reeling from the blow. I had been running wildly to catch a softball, and had run a little too far. The ball whipped back my glove and socked me in the face.

At the hospital, I gripped my mother's hand as the specialist set my broken nose. The pain was unbearable, and blood ran freely. An hour later, shaking and still in pain, I climbed off the chair with a cast on my nose.

A few weeks later, I eagerly removed the cast. Surely my nose would be nice and straight again. But-oh! I stared at the mirror in disbelief. I could not deny that my nose was still slightly crooked.

It's not fair! I stormed inwardly, swallowing the tears that threatened to come. *I went through all this torture for nothing! And next week is my cochlear implant surgery, which will add a scar to my blemishes. I have all these deformities at only sixteen!*

Being a woman, I long for beauty. I don't have flawless features, but I still want to appear attractive. I like to feel neatly and pleasantly attired. Beauty is important to me.

This small incident had a big impact on my life. Yes, my nose is slightly crooked (at least, I think it is). But a crooked nose has no power to detract from the real kind of beauty, that which shines from within. My physical body is only a container for my spirit, and it matters not if my body isn't perfect. What is important is my spirit. Am I beautiful inside?

Just as I put a premium on taking care of my body, so I should take pains to ensure that the things of my spirit are taken care of. Are my attitudes, perspectives, motives, and ideals beautiful? Do I cultivate Christian graces and virtues? Do I let Jesus fill me with His sweetness?

When I suffer, it can ruin me or it can evoke an inner loveliness. When I lie crushed and bleeding before God, I can allow Him to mold me into His image. Hanging desperately onto God, I can become more like Him.

I know that I will never have stunningly beautiful features. Outward beauty I can do without. Still, I ask God to fill me with His presence. Jesus can make me beautiful inside.

Belizean Beauty?

READ: Psalm 90:14-17

Warning: You can't visit Belize without losing your factory perfect, fresh from the mold appearance.

In the morning you may carefully comb and spray your hair, but by evening it might slightly resemble a lion's mane. Wisps will fly in the wind when you ride in the bed of a pickup truck. Humidity will make your hair frizz—more than you knew it could! And the heat and dirt will definitely make it greasy.

During rainy season, your dresses may get splattered, stained, or even soaked as you travel. Mud will shod your feet and cling to your ankles. In fact, you probably won't clean the dirt from under your toenails until you come back to the States.

Mosquitoes love American blood. Their bites will polka dot your arms and legs. If those bites become infected, they'll swell, turn red, and ooze.

Dry season will bring dust. It will roll in billows from passing trucks. It will make your face grimy and turn your white veilings brown. Dry season will mean heat…and sweat.

I've experienced it! Helplessly, I found myself stripped of any superficial beauty. There I was, meeting new people and making first impressions. What did I look like?

Frizzled, sweated, and muddy, I suddenly realized that the only place left for me to be beautiful was inside.

But, along with all the dirt and dust in Belize, I found women who were truly beautiful. Wives were content with tiny gas refrigerators and beans and rice. Belizean women clung to God even when their husbands slid into sin. Mothers cheerfully served God in front of gas stoves, wringer washers, and dishpans. Busy mission workers paused to visit with and care about me.

Oh yes, their hair got messy and their dresses got stained, just like mine did. But their beauty was in deeper things. They had beautiful spirits. They were content, faithful, joyful, and caring. They were beautiful where it really counts.

Where is our beauty?

Wrinkles on My Heart

READ: Hebrews 12:12-15

I sometimes worry about getting wrinkles on my face. Oh, I know I can expect to develop lines. It's all in the process of aging. *But what if I develop premature wrinkles?* I whisper as I eye my forehead in the mirror. I check out the tiny lines by the outer corners of my eyes that appear when I squint. I'm sure that my eyes will be all crinkly around the edges if I spend many more days out on the range! So I rub on more cold cream.

I just don't want to look like an old woman before my time, I guess. I want to take care of my skin, keep it moistened in this dry climate.

I've been realizing, though, that any wrinkle on my face

is very minor compared to a more serious place I could get them: on my heart.

I'm not talking about a physical occurrence of lines. Far deeper and deadlier, the ugly wrinkles of bitterness are often where the smoothness of love and forgiveness should be.

This is when a quote from J. Garfield is a challenge to me:

> "Let wrinkles
> be written
> on our brows
> and not
> on our hearts."

I talked once with a woman who used to run a home for elderly people. She said the same old people who were so sweet and dear when there were visitors were almost impossible to work with after the visitors left. These were the people, she explained, who put on a good front to the world all their lives. On the inside and to those close to them, bitterness raged.

"What you are now is what you'll become—even more so!"

Yes, I want to become a sweet old lady. Sweet to the very core of my heart. And it starts now. When my heart wants to get ugly and I notice tiny beginnings of bitterness, I need to apply God's cold cream of love to smooth out those wrinkles.

And when I look in the mirror and I think I see the beginnings of a wrinkle on my face, I will see it not as a worry, but as a reminder.

I'd rather have it there than on my heart.

Lessons From a Lavender

READx: Colossians 1:9-11

Come join me! I'm relaxing and enjoying the colors in our perennial bed—lavender beside black-eyed susans. Let me slide over; this bench is certainly long enough for two. There, that's better.

Do you like the plant lavender? I admire it. Sure, I like its gray-green foliage and dusty purple flower spikes, but there's more than that.

I want a character like lavender. Lavender is a gentle flower. Compare it with this clump of black-eyed susans beside our bench. Although the yellow black-eyed susans overpower the subtle purple, the lavender quietly produces its own beauty. That's my prayer: that we would be content to bloom within the circumstances God's given us. And continue to bloom, even if no one notices. Know what I mean?

Lavender's most beautiful quality is its scent. Here, have a spike. Press it between your fingers. See! As you crush it, it releases a richer fragrance.

Isn't that a beautiful lesson? Only God can give us the grace to radiate His love when we're irritated. Only He can give us a song when our hearts our bleeding. But He can do it!

Don't you long to have a character like lavender? I do. I'm going to slip a little into my pocket as a reminder. Here, would you like a sprig too?

Let's ask God to make us gentle, quiet, content, radiating His love, singing His joy—beautiful to the root.

Me? Tall?

READ: Isaiah 64:8; Romans 9:20,21

The man adjusted the sombrero on his head. "Your daughter is very tall," he told my dad. "How old is she?"

"Sixteen," Dad replied.

"Sixteen!" the man exclaimed. He looked up at me and shook his head incredulously. "She is *very* tall."

I had learned that Mexican people said and did unexpected things. The man's statement shouldn't have taken me by surprise, but it did. You see, I'm barely over five feet tall. When I recovered from my shock, I surprised the man by saying, "In the States, I'm short."

"You don't say so," the Mexican shook his head.

I looked at the sparkling water of the Vera Cruz harbor and thought of a story I had read. I could almost picture Amy Carmichael stepping onto the shore of India. As a child, she had longed for blue eyes, even prayed that God would suddenly make her eyes turn blue. Her disappointment was keen when she looked in the mirror and saw that her eyes were still brown.

Years later, she answered God's call to India. One of her first thoughts when she stood on the dock in India was, "These people have brown eyes like me." She was thankful God hadn't answered her childhood prayer.

As I stood beside a dock in Mexico, I felt a kinship with Amy Carmichael. I thought of all those times that I had wished I were a few inches taller. I smiled at the thought and looked at the short Mexicans all around me. I was glad I didn't tower above everyone.

Did you ever notice how many short people wish they

were taller, and how many tall people wish they were shorter? Why is it so hard to be satisfied with the way God made us? Perhaps it is because we lose sight of God. We forget that He knows everything, including what physical characteristics would fit best with His plan for our lives. We forget that He always wants the best for us. We forget that He's in control.

What can we do to change our appearance? Nothing! What can we do to change our attitude? A lot! The first step is to realize that God has planned our lives. When we submit to that plan, we accept ourselves the way God made us.

Thank You, Lord, for the wonderful variety You have created. Help us to focus on being in the center of Your will instead of wishing we were different. Thank You, too, that You do what You know will be good for us, even when we don't like it. Help us to be satisfied with Your perfect plan for our lives—and our appearance!

The Treasure

READ: Psalm 149:1-6

There is a treasure of infinite value, only to be revealed to those who search for it. When a woman finds it, she will never lack God's richest blessings. Some have found it, and have prospered. Others are still searching. Many are sitting in their houses, idle. They have no desire to search, to find, to inherit this priceless treasure.

I am searching for this treasure. Every day the search becomes more intense, more personal. I struggle to obtain this treasure because I am human—I am so quick to defend myself, to be impatient and outspoken. I'm tempted to be disrespectful of authority, disobedient, and selfish. I can become self-sufficient, self-seeking, self-loving. When I indulge in these things, I cannot have the treasure.

What is this treasure? First Peter three, verse four tells us. "But let it be the hidden man of the heart, in that which is not corruptible, even the ornament of a meek and quiet spirit, which is in the sight of God of great price."

There it is. A meek and quiet spirit. An ornament of transcendent worth.

Meekness is defined as "not inclined to anger or resentment, pliant, gentle, mild, humble." Quietness is an inner rest and total submission to God. A meek and quiet spirit can only be obtained by an intimate relationship with God.

Having a meek and quiet spirit doesn't mean being backward, silent, and somber. It means *trusting* in Him, and resting in His perfect peace. It lies in allowing Jesus to fill me with humility, tenderness, and uncircumstantial joy. It is found in acceptance of His will for my life.

Those who have secured this treasure are rich. Those who have not will perish. Those who search will find. God will bestow on them His meek and quiet spirit, which is, in His sight, of great price.

My Wedding Dress

READ: Jeremiah 2:32,33; Isaiah 61:10

One day as we were house cleaning, I came across an article on June brides. One comment that impressed me was that more emphasis is put on the dress of the bride than anything else. As I went on about my work I thought about this. A lot of emphasis, sometimes too much emphasis, is put on the bride's dress: what kind of material, how it was made and more.

Then, I thought, *Just how much emphasis do I place on preparing my eternal wedding dress so that it is the pure white garment which the Groom (the Lord Jesus Christ) would value? Am I ready so that when the Groom makes His appearance He will take me as His bride? Are my garments fit to wear when I stand beside Him?*

Every bride wants to have a nice dress. Doesn't the Lord deserve just as much? When Jesus returns, He will not be looking at earthly clothes, but at my spiritual robe. Does it have black ugly spots and little holes and tears? Is Jesus going to receive a bride in a dress that is whiter than snow? Or, is His bride going to be waiting in a tattered garment not fit for any bride, let alone a King's?

I mentioned having holes in my dress. Well I don't want a wedding dress like that. I would want a nice, neat dress that had been carefully sewn. But guess what! Jesus has offered to sew my dress for that exciting, glorious day. He can do it better than any earthly seamstress.

Sometimes, however, I get the idea that I know how to do it better than God. I try to take over, and that causes problems. I sew a wrong seam here and snag it there. Once the dress looks ugly, I hand it back to Jesus. In tears, I ask Him to take over. Sadly, though He may fix the tear and make a new seam, there will always be a scar or small hole. It may be almost invisible, but it's still there. The garment is no longer neat, but marred.

That calls something else to my attention. When I take over, causing ugly marks like snags and rips, it brings shame to the One who sewed it. When I fail, it causes a stumbling block for others and damages the Lord's reputation. Maybe someone was going to give their heart to the Lord, but because of my mistake they decided against it.

I want to allow the Lord to prepare my wedding dress and do what He wants with my life. His way, not my way, will keep away the snags and mistakes that would ruin the looks of my soul. I want Him to be pleased when I'm presented as part of His bride.

The Virtuous Young Woman

READ: Proverbs 31:10-31

Who can find a virtuous young woman? For her price is far above rubies.

The heart of her parents safely trusts in her, and she satisfies their needs.

She will not hinder them, but help them all the days of her life.

She finds durable fabric, and busily sews useful garments for the family.

When she buys groceries for the household, she makes wise selections.

She rises up early to prepare breakfast and plan the day's work.

She considers a product carefully. If it will benefit the family, she buys it for a good price.

She is energetic, a hard worker, and watches for bargains. She works far into the night.

She sews for the poor, and gives generously to the needy.

She has no fear of winter for her household, for she has helped to make warm clothes for all of them.

She makes beautiful, neat clothing for herself, clothing that is simple and glorifies God.

Her father is well known, for he is busy with the work of the church.

She makes or grows fine products and sells them.

When she speaks, her words are wise, and kindness is the rule for everything she says.

She watches carefully all that goes on in her household, and is never lazy.

Her family stands and blesses her, especially her parents.

There are many virtuous young women, but this woman excels them all.

Charm and popularity are deceptive, and beauty doesn't last, but a young woman who reverences and obeys God shall be greatly praised.

She shall be rewarded for her sacrificial work, and even the leaders will praise her in the end.

Just Joking!

"Hey, we should play a joke on Anita and Dora," I whispered to my friends. "See, here they come." We watched as our two friends walked toward us. Our former teacher had invited us for an afternoon of games. Waiting for enough people to play volleyball, we chatted by the roadside.

"Well, what shall we do?" one whispered back.

My teasing nature was up. That's when I'm dangerous to be with! "Let's ignore them completely," I suggested, "and then after a while, we'll start copycatting everything they say."

"Karen, but don't you think they'll get mad at us?"

"Oh, no. You know how Anita is. She likes that kind of stuff. She teases lots herself."

When Anita and Dora walked up to us we pretended to ignore them. Seeing this, Anita and Dora crossed the street, and went to the store. I started getting worried. My plan didn't seem so great after all.

It wasn't. Anita and Dora took our joke seriously. Anita, who was my classmate and a very good friend, didn't talk to me. I didn't know it would affect her so deeply. But it did, and I had a hard time getting her to talk to me again. I said several times: "But, Anita, I was only joking!"

Finally after several agonizing hours, she told me, "I forgive you, but please don't joke like that again."

I assured her I had learned my lesson. My stupid joke had spoiled the whole afternoon. I didn't enjoy the game. Flashbacks of things I regretted doing appeared before me. I felt like a miserable Christian. All because of a joke.

Are jokes worth it? Was mine? The answer is plain: NO. Why did I risk losing a friendship because I wanted to play a joke and act smart? I thought Anita wouldn't be hurt. She was. Yes, even Anita, who is the life of the party.

I know some jokes are okay, but some of them hurt. If I hurt my friends, am I being Christ-like? Does that draw them to Jesus? After all, if my friends know Jesus lives in me, and then I hurt them with a joke, will they have a desire to be like me?

Now, I try to be more careful about jokes. Friendships aren't worth losing by just joking.

Greater Than Stone Face

READ: Proverbs 12:5; 23:5-7

The Great Stone Face was merely a heap of rocks on the mountainside. But Ernest, the lad of Hawthorne's story, knew it was more. If one viewed them from the valley, the stones looked like an enormous face.

Born and raised under the gaze of this Great Stone Face, Ernest loved to study the face glowing with wisdom, gentleness, and strength of character. Prophecy said that someday a man who looked just like the Stone Face would come to the valley. Ernest longed to meet the man.

One day a rumor drifted into the valley. Gossip said that

a wealthy merchant who was returning to the valley looked exactly like the Great Stone Face. With the neighborhood, Ernest anticipated the merchant's arrival.

But Ernest was disappointed. The merchant lacked the kindness and nobility of the face on the mountain.

More rumors sprouted. Three more times Ernest was disappointed. These men, called twins of the Stone Face, were shallow and greedy. The Great Stone Face was rich with kindness, wisdom, and humility.

Eventually, Ernest himself fulfilled the prophecy. As a visiting poet listened to his wisdom, the poet realized that this humble man bore the image of the Great Stone Face. Ernest had focused on the Face and absorbed its qualities for so long that he actually looked like it.

Hawthorne illustrated a fact. We become like that on which we focus. Those things that we think about all day become part of our character.

God knew this before Hawthorne did. That's why He tells us in Philippians 4:8, "Whatsoever things are true...whatsoever things are pure, whatsoever things are lovely, whatsoever things are of good report...think on these things."

Many things distract our focus.

We focus on our clothing, our hairstyles, our actions, and ourselves. We grow proud and self-centered.

We compare ourselves with our friends. "I'm not like them," we say, and crawl into a homemade prison of inferiority.

We become distracted by a hectic lifestyle. Jobs, chorus programs, and youth activities leave us frazzled.

God has an answer for us. "Come," he invites. "Look at the things that are lovely and pure. Focus on the true, the honest, and the noble. Quit looking at earth's scum."

Our lives will radiate the One on whom we focus. His

loveliness will glow in our spirits. His gentleness will mellow our touch. His wisdom will strengthen our decisions.

God calls us to focus on Him, because He is greater than any Stone Face.

Quality Christians

READ: Matthew 7:15-29

I fingered the material carefully, dreaming of the beautiful dress that could be sewn with it. It looked like a strong, comfortable piece of fabric. Even though it cost a bit more than I usually paid, I was sure it would be worth the extra money.

I took the material home and sewed it as soon as possible. After I finished it, I wore it and was quite pleased with the result. It fit perfectly and it was comfortable.

But something happened. After I washed my new dress, it shrank to about one half of the original size! How disappointed I was! All the money and time I had put into that dress was wasted. I realized that this material was exactly the opposite of what I had thought it to be. It was of no value.

Many people today are like my material was. On the outside, they appear to be some of the best Christians around. They are active members of the church, Sunday school teachers, and mission supporters. They often lead in public prayer and attend all church activities. Every Sunday, they come to church dressed in their proper attire and wish everyone God's blessing.

Yet what would one see in that person's life during the week? When they, like the material, are dipped in hot water, their characteristics change. Instead of reading their Bible through the week and seeking God's will for their lives, the first thing they do in the morning is read the newspaper. Instead of praying, they gossip for hours on the telephone about their neighbors and fellow church members.

Wouldn't an onlooker be disappointed to find this in a Christian's life? Let's be quality Christians—not only on Sunday, but also throughout the whole week.

The Chambered Nautilus
(An allegory)

READ: James 1:2,12; 1 Peter 4:12

Deep in the ocean, amid a wilderness of waving seaweed, beady-eyed fish, and slimy algae, lay a tiny creature. Just born into a fearful ocean world, it shrank into its shell, afraid of the sharp seaweed and flopping fish. Cringing at the cold, slippery algae, it timidly wondered, "Can I survive life in the ocean?"

The chambered nautilus struggled with fear. Day after day, terrifying creatures threatened its safety. After retreating into its shell frequently, the nautilus began to take courage. "This isn't so bad, I can face this!" it thought ambitiously. Lifting its head, the nautilus drew a wall of pearl behind it, and moved on.

An exciting era emerged. Waves splashed joyously,

dissolving into silly, giggling ripples. The seaweed stopped whipping its sharp blades at its neighbors. Crabby creatures quit eating their siblings. Groggy fish went to bed and slept. Waking up refreshed, they ceased their senseless flopping and took lessons in the art of graceful swimming. The nautilus was bursting with brilliant potential, and its chamber expanded. Still, it had to close the door, and face the future.

Angry waves slapped with malicious fury. Changing overnight, the sweet-tempered seaweed turned bitter and slashed passersby cruelly. Furiously fighting with others and itself, it shredded to angry bits. The fishes threw temper tantrums, ate their siblings and bit their parents. Sneering and spitting, they called the nautilus names and spread horrible stories. Anguished, the nautilus lived in constant terror of being destroyed completely by his vile companions. "Should I retaliate, or should I give up totally?" it agonized. No, it could not do either. The nautilus knew that it must draw the silvery curtain of pearl behind it, and once again leave the past.

Darkness fell. A heavy shroud hung over the ocean. Black waters hid any life or emotion. Sea animals slunk into murky corners. The seaweed wilted. The nautilus was caught in the awful void of loneliness. No one spoke. No one moved. Days dragged by in heavy silence. Finally, the time arrived. The chambered nautilus sighed, and slowly closed the door.

Years came and went. The time came when the nautilus' work was done, and the pearly shell lay on the golden beach. Spiraling behind him, the shell spoke vividly of battles waged, youthful idealism, dreadful loneliness, and finally sweet submission. Those years of toil created these pearly chambers, each chamber larger and more beautiful than the last.

Chapter 7

Love
at Home

Sibling Struggles

READ: 1 Peter 3:8-12

Horrified, I read back over some journal entries from my early teen years. Had I really acted like that? I didn't remember those incidents. Then I realized that those were some of the same things that I was condemning my younger sister for doing. How easily I had forgotten the struggles of my younger years.

My sister needs someone to understand and to encourage her, not to judge her. In order to improve my relationship with her, I must first improve my relationship with God. Then I will be able to develop my friendship with my sister.

I need to get rid of the attitude that I'm better than she is. I may be more mature in some areas, but that doesn't mean I'm better than she is. Praying for her will also improve my attitude.

It's important that I take the time to talk with her. Through this I can discern her struggles and frustrations, and can share how I faced those same struggles.

As an older sister, I need to be a good example. Will I lead her to Christ or away from Him?

My sister is a special blessing, and I must remember not to take her for granted.

When I Needed a Sister

READ: John 16:23-27

Sobs woke me up late that December night. My eyelids popped open and I sat up in bed. "What's wrong?" I called across the room to my five-year-old sister.

"My ear..." she sniffed as I knelt beside her bed. "It hurts."

I spent the next several minutes rubbing her back and praying for her, wishing I could be in my own bed. But I told myself not to complain, because *for this sister I prayed.*

Sometimes I have a hard time understanding God's timetables.

You see, I really *needed* a sister eight, maybe ten, years ago. I enjoyed my brothers a lot, but longed for the companionship of a sister. Someone to whisper secrets to, someone to share a bedroom with, someone to take my side against the boys in childish skirmishes. I waited, and waited, and waited. At last, when I was fourteen, my first sister was born. A couple years later, another one arrived.

Wow! Thanks, God! *Two* answers to my childhood prayers. They were (and continue to be) such joys. I was thrilled, but as the years passed, I was also puzzled.

Hadn't God waited too long? Weren't fourteen years too many years to have between sisters? I didn't really *need* them now. I was outgrowing little girl stuff, and they were too young to share my heart with or fill up lonely hours. Long ago, a sister to me meant someone who would be my comrade, someone to borrow dresses from, someone to play dolls and "house" with. But I didn't have any sisters then.

Now, in reality, a sister is someone who chatters nonstop

when I need quiet, someone who hides my most essential toiletries, someone who is always wanting to play games with me, someone who watches me intently and imitates my every word and action. (Ever notice how ridiculous it looks to see a toddler do or say something that seemed so "cool" to you?)

Well, God doesn't always look at it the same way I do. He doesn't always give me what I want; He gives me what I need. In this case, I believe He met my needs by supplying for my want. He answered my prayer for a sister later because He knew there were lessons I would need to learn. Now, sharing my room (and drawers and closets!) with my little sisters is a molding experience. I don't always like it, but I can't resist it, knowing that God wants to shape my character.

From where I'm sitting I can see a little doll with a broken leg lying on the floor. Other toys and shoes remind me that my room is not my own. Then I look up to the windowsill. I see a bouquet of purple and yellow wildflowers there. They're a bit wilted now, but a few days ago, God's little answer to my girlhood prayers brought them to me. And I am thankful.

Sisters

READx: Mark 3:33-35

I'm the only girl in a family of boys. You know how brothers can be: aggravating, teasing, annoying, irritating, and the list goes on! Now, can you imagine me, a little girl with four big brothers just doing anything to pull out those tears? Well, they accomplished it many times. Alone in my room, the tears would rush out as I'd ask myself, "Why do I have to be the only girl? Dear God, please give me a sister."

My eyes envisioned my room with a double bed, extra dresses, and most of all, a little sister to fill them up. I longed to feel her arms around me, bidding me good night. At night, I'd pretend I was talking to my unknown sister. I'd tell her what had happened during the day. Problems would spill out to the unseen ears.

I believe it was hardest when I saw poems, cards, mugs, and so many other things about sisters. When some of my friends went out on special trips just with their sisters, I wished for one to present poems to or spend times with.

Other people would tell me that I'm lucky to be the only girl. I acted like, "Yeah, it's nice. You're right, it's fun." But deep down, I said, "No! You just try it sometime and see what it's like. Try it first—then tell me."

Little by little, I realized I'm not the only one that doesn't have a sister to cuddle up to at bedtime, chat about friends, and tell her what's on my heart. My grandmother was the only girl in her family. She must have gone through it herself. She told my brothers to "take care of Karen".

I admit that being the only girl in the family has brought its good things, too. I have my own room. I find that a real blessing that not all enjoy. I can have my personal devotions in privacy. A sister won't come banging in when I'd want to be by myself.

My brothers are very special to me. I get to spend more time with them. It seems to me that I'm special to them too, since I'm their only little sister. Some girls don't even have brothers. That must be strange. Can you imagine no brothers to tease you?! Must be a bit quiet!

Other kinds of sisters have come into my life. Special friends have to be the replacements. My brothers have provided me with sisters-in-law. They do a fine job of treating me as a sister. And my dear Salvadoran sisters in the church are very understanding. "Thank you, God, for the many sisters you have given me."

If you have a sister, thank God for her. Not everyone has the blessing you have. Please enjoy her!

Love

READ: 1 Corinthians 13

Love is wiping up the just-washed floor after your brother tracked mud all over it. It is patiently scrubbing stains in your dress that your sister borrowed. It is getting a drink for your little brother for the sixth time.

Love is cheerfully performing dull tasks. It is not seeking praise, or crediting yourself for good deeds. It is doing your best without expecting anything in return.

Love is deferring to the wishes of others. It is staying home with the family even when you long for a break. It is following the wishes of authority, and doing even more than what is required. Love is not desperate for its own way.

Love is kind. It is offering compliments for jobs well done. Love is believing in others, and sharing in their suffering, even though it means opening your heart to pain. Love is not talking only of yourself, it is not superior. It is listening to other's point of view, and when a storm of words passes, it gently separates the chaff from the wheat. It is not fastening yourself to someone well-liked, to pursue popularity. Love does not desire to be noticed. Love is unselfish, and still gives when there is nothing left to give.

Love grows slowly. It is not the rush of feeling, the quick beating heart, the self-conscious blush. It does not spurt wildly, then wilt. Love is an unconscious blossoming. It is not dependent on circumstances. It does not make you act unnatural, or appear bright when your heart is heavy. Love is stable, and urges spiritual growth. It flows directly from the King of Love.

Love is a decision. Love is eternal. Many waters cannot quench love.

Diamonds in the Rough

READ: Matthew 18:2-6

It's sometimes hard to recognize them as diamonds. Their edges are rough, they're often dirty, and by their appearance, they could hardly pass as diamonds.

But yet they are.

They hang about the house—inconveniencing me, frustrating me, and annoying me. They don't act like diamonds.

But yet they are.

Right now they're irritating me. I'm sitting in front of our house, trying to catch some early spring rays and writing this. They're playing ball, insisting on playing ball, too close to the house (and me). I've nearly been hit twice and feel about as comfortable as a cat in a room full of rocking chairs.

They're diamonds in the rough, all right.

Siblings can be so downright bothersome, often puzzling, and sometimes very honest. At the time of this writing, I teach grades one through five in our little schoolhouse here on the ranch. It's awkward balancing the role of teacher/ sister. Once, when things just weren't going well, I decided we must do some evaluating. So I asked my pupils what I should do to be a better teacher. Their answers were revealing: "Be more patient. Don't get disgusted. Don't be grouchy."

I think I know what I need to work on. And I think I could do well to carry that advice from the role of "teacher" to the one of "sister."

What big sister hasn't been impatient? ("Hurry up so we can finish!") Or disgusted? ("Come on, can't you do better than that?") Or grouchy? ("Leave me alone, I just woke up.")

Can I overlook my sibling's mistakes, their imperfections, their childish ways? Can't I love them in spite of sticky hands, dirty sinks, and rude burps? Yes! After all, I am a diamond in the rough myself. God isn't finished working on me yet. He surely will make all things beautiful in HIS time.

I must do better. I must be patient, pleasant, interested in their lives. I cannot brush them aside like pesky mosquitoes. They're God's jewels and they're very precious in their own unique way. The Bible teaches us to look to them as our examples, to believe with the simplicity they do. "For of such," said Jesus, "is the kingdom of God" (Mark 10:14).

Kiss Me!

READ: Ephesians 4:30-32

Up and down, through the living room door, then dashing out the opening on the opposite side, right through the schoolroom. Oops! There went a chair, still they don't slacken their pace. My little brothers are having a free-for-all at the peril of all who get in their way.

About that time big sister comes on the scene. She snaps, "STOP, Boys," but to no avail. Now they are not only chasing each other, but they are also teasing their sister. She either stands there exasperated or tries chasing them, which only adds to the din.

Why do little brothers have to be so exasperating? For one thing, they have a carnal nature (just like their sisters). And, if they have an opportunity to get their sisters up in the air about something, why not take it?

Once, when my little brother was trying our patience, my sister asked him what he really wanted.

He responded, "A kiss."

Ouch!! Maybe I am the problem, not showing them enough love. How many times do I snap at my brothers when I could've kept quiet or talked to them nicely? Could I cause them to be wayward someday because of my un-Christ-like reactions?

Oh, that I could watch my tongue! Some time ago I found a poem about a child who was nice, gentle, and a pleasure to be with in public, but even more so at home. I long for that quality too.

Jesus, help me watch my tongue and actions. Please help me to always be sweet and talk nicely to my brothers even when they don't do what I wish they would. I want to edify and not destroy their characters. In Jesus Name, Amen.

My Brother Has a Girlfriend

READ: Philippians 1:9-11

"Yup, she's my girlfriend now," Tim answered with a grin.

"Congratulations!" I shouted, really excited about it. Now I could tease him and play all kinds of jokes on him and Sonia.

That's how it all started. Announcement, excitement, and...sharing. Yes, sharing my brother with Sonia. And I still wanted a BIG part of his life—sharing time, talks, and just being together. Now he had started spending his time with Sonia, and I got the leftovers.

I didn't like it. Chaperoning reminded me of my new relationship with both of them. I felt like an intruder whenever the three of us were together. I zipped my lips. I didn't want Tim to know I was unhappy. I didn't want him to know I was jealous. I didn't want him to know that I felt left out, not only by him, but by the other couples in the youth group too. I wanted to be happy for Tim, but I pitied myself. Feeling mixed up, I'd cry again. And I wouldn't tell Tim.

One evening, after the youth meeting, I was talking with Sonia and another girl, when another one came along and said that she wanted to talk to all the couples. So, I had to leave. I was not impressed. Why had they put me out? I went home and cried. I resolved I was going to talk with Tim.

I could hardly talk, but somehow Tim understood. He let me talk, then explained things to me in a way that let me know he cared about my feelings. I began to see things from a different perspective.

Now I understand that Tim loves me as his sister in a

different way than he loves Sonia. Even if he has a girlfriend, he needs a sister. I'm glad Tim's my brother, and brotherly love will never end!

No Tacos

READ: Proverbs 1:7-9

Oh, just to eat some *real* tacos again! Mexican tacos! The last three times I went to the States, I flew instead of going by land. The trouble is that when I fly over Mexico, I don't get to eat their wonderful tacos. So, when I heard of an opportunity to go to the Mexican border, I jumped for it.

You see, Papa and my brothers Tim and Paul had car trouble while traveling through Mexico. Tim came on home. He and another brother, Philip, decided to go get the disabled vehicle at the Mexican/Guatemalan border and meet Papa and Paul.

When I heard of it, the thought of traveling with my brothers and eating tacos told me I also wanted to go. Soon, we were driving along, talking of many things. We saw at least one accident along the way. We talked about death.

A little thought popped into my head, *What if we'd get to an accident, and it'd be Papa or Paul?* I quickly dismissed the thought, reminding myself that what I imagine usually doesn't come true.

Suddenly, ahead of us, we saw lights flashing, a pickup in a ditch, and a crowd of people. When we saw Paul's pickup parked along the side of the road, we knew the wrecked one was Papa's.

Panic gripped my heart, knowing that Papa had been in an accident. "Oh, God, please help us!" I cried out in desperation.

Just then, a man came and told me everything was okay, not to worry. I saw Papa, his shirt streaked with blood, sitting on the bank. The police rushed him off to the hospital, along with the drunk who had swerved in front of him.

After the tow-truck had lugged away the unfortunate Chevy and its thrown-off camper, I leaned back against Philip's pickup and gazed at a beautiful palm tree swaying in the breeze. I thought of how close the steering wheel and the seat were smashed together. Papa could have easily been killed if he hadn't been so thin.

Philip came along. "It just makes me appreciate Papa all the more," I said to him.

Really, I have to think of all the times when I haven't honored my father like I should. After his kidnapping, I thought I would always appreciate him. But, as a normal teenager, it wasn't so easy sometimes.

However, after seeing him saved like that, seeing him in pain, seeing him weak and fragile, I realized how much I loved my father. I'm fortunate to have him.

I didn't get to eat tacos after all, but that didn't matter. What did matter was my new attitude toward my father. Tacos will be my reminder.

Chapter 8

Therefore Give Us Love

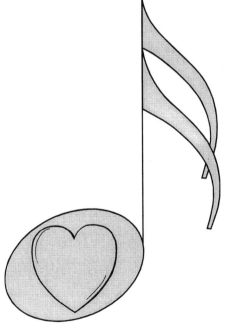

Perfect Love

READ: 1 John 4:16-19

Fear tugged at my heart as I walked through the labyrinths of white hospital walls, around looming metal machines on the Diagnostic Imaging floor.

The nurse stopped, and pointed to the adjacent room. "You can go in there," she said with a friendly smile. "Please remove anything metal that you might be wearing."

My fingers trembled as I pulled out hairpins and removed my implant processor. Now I was ready for the X-ray that would determine if I needed to undergo another surgery.

I was experiencing that cold, numbing dread that we call *fear*. I am human, and inevitably, I wage battles with fear. Fear of the present, fear of the future, fear of the unknown.

Yet, in the chilling realms of fear, there is a warm Presence, a loving Shepherd. I run to Him, and in His arms I find safety, security, and unfailing love.

That perfect love casts out all fear.

My Lover, My Lord

READ: 1 John 4:1-10

Are you looking for the love of your life? Look no longer! Do you desire someone who will listen to your every word and not loose interest in you? Stop looking! Do you wish to build a friendship with someone that will last forever? Please cease glancing around you!

Look up!

Girls like to dream and hope for the future. But although there are many nice fellows out there, we will never find the "perfect" one.

So, before we enter any kind of human relationship, we should develop our relationship with the greatest Lover of all—Jesus. This is the time of our lives to let Him "court" us. He loves us so much, and so many times we just ignore Him! What girl would ignore her boyfriend? What girl would ignore her greatest Lover, Jesus?

He's been watching us, courting us for years. He wonders why we do not put Him first in our lives when He has done so much for us. We rarely acknowledge His gifts—nature, family, health, light, love, and laughter. We don't talk to Him nearly as much as many girls do to their boyfriends.

The advantages of being His beloved are enormous. No one will tell you to quit dreaming about Him. (By the way, His thoughts toward *you* are more in number than the sand! Psalm 139:17,18) No complaining about short notes; His love letters run 66 books long and have 1,189 chapters. Have you finished reading them yet?

It's delightful to be courted by such a God, to exchange secrets, confidences, and notes of love. Have you written a love letter to Him recently?

Dear Lord, only You can satisfy the yearnings of my heart. Only You can answer my "why's." I give my life anew to You, in this beautiful relationship with You. You are LOVE and I thank You for loving me. Thank You for never giving up on me, even when I want to pursue other loves. Your love is always there—faithful, never-ending.

God, You are and always will be the Greatest Lover I will ever have. No one but You can understand the joy we have in communing together. Sometimes I can almost feel that You "joy over me with singing" (Zephaniah 3:17). That quiet understanding brings peace. I love You!

Genuine Love

READ: Proverbs 16:20-23

Several years ago, I read an article* on premature romances that contained some good advice that has helped me during my teenage years. Maybe you're asking some questions and want some answers. Here are some for you from that article.

Question #1: "Is it right for me to let my attraction for a person of the opposite sex be known?

"What do you gain by letting anybody know? Absolutely nothing! It is only natural to feel this attraction. God made you like that. And if the Lord wills, some day it will be right and good for you to have a special friend, and to marry. But until that day arrives, do yourself the favor of guarding it to yourself.

"When I was young, in our youth group there was a lovely girl named Eunice. Several of us fellows liked her. But she was smart. She never let us know whom she liked. She was equally friendly with all the boys. Do you know what that did? It made us respect her more. She was no free-for-all."

Questions #2: "Should I forget the attraction I feel?

"Hardly. The attraction is normal. What you should do is give this attraction to God. That way, you will avoid being a slave to it. You can then rest in knowing that He will guard your treasure. If sometime He would give this treasure back, He will show you at that time."

"When Eunice was young, she did have a secret preference. She never forgot it as such. But she had it in its right place.

"I was not that mature. I fell in love all over for Eunice. Everybody knew about it. But I well remember the day I got sick and tired of all the problems involved in premature romances. I knelt beside the bed and prayed something like this: 'Father, I'm giving You this love I feel. If she is for me, You'll keep her. Help me to be free to serve You.'

"Sure it was hard to put that prayer to practice, but I found victory. In my case I never did quite forget her, and I never will. She is now my wife!"

Conclusion: "If you have a love you can't forget, just give it to Jesus. He'll take care of it for you.

"Dedicate yourself to knowing Jesus. Dedicate yourself to developing a mature Christian life. If later God gives you a love, maybe even the same one you gave to His trust before, you will be prepared to have a good courtship and a marriage that is beautiful. That will then not be called a premature romance, but a genuine love from God.

* "Premature Romances"
by Pablo Yoder.
Used by permission

Filled Up

READ: Psalm 16

If you struggle with infatuation, you have a void in your life that needs to be filled.

Fill your life with God! It is not enough to take something away that does not belong; you cannot live on nothing. Open your heart to God! Discover the fullness and security that He offers. Enter into a close relationship with Him. Memorize Scripture and let His Word penetrate you. Spend time in meditation and honest prayer, and cultivate the fruits of the Spirit in your life. God loves and understands you as no human can!

Enjoy your family. They are the most precious people God has given you. God designed your family to help you and provide security for you. Your home has a rich store of parental wisdom, rallying support, and emotional fulfillment. Your family accepts you just as you are. Take time to enjoy your family—the rewards are great!

Get involved with others. Instead of focusing so sharply on yourself, notice the needs around you. There's always somebody that needs an encouraging note, a little gift, a word of kindness, help with some little task, or a friendly smile. Focus on the multiplying needs around you. Give the world the best you have, and the best will come back to you.

Pursue some creative impulse. Take a writing course, art lessons, or craft classes. Let your mother teach you how to braid rugs, knit, and crochet. Sew for a busy mother. Write inspirational stories and articles. Create cards to give away. Find something that you enjoy doing, and use that God-given talent well.

Indeed, when your heart is occupied with God, your family, and the needs around you, you will find that it has been filled, and is overflowing!

If You Love Something

READ: Lamentations 3:24-33

Bible Institute is my favorite place to be. There I meet with my dear Christian friends. But, this year I had a wrong motive hidden in my heart. I wanted to see more of a certain young man, a friend of mine named Pablo. I knew very well that it wasn't the Lord who prompted this feeling.

We had written letters to each other until Daddy found out. He spent time talking to both of us. He told us we were too young for a special friendship, and that we shouldn't talk together much.

It seemed so hard to resist the temptation. Since we couldn't talk, we wrote things in a notebook and exchanged notebooks when we met at a youth activity or something.

When Bible Institute finally came, it was everything I'd hoped for—friends, fellowship, and inspiring classes, AND Pablo. I don't remember which day or at what time, but I began to feel that my life needed an "overhaul." I felt it all through that day. In the evening, I stood to take counseling.

I went with two others who had stood, told them my predicament, and how I felt about it. Then, one of them gave this suggestion: "I think it goes back to this saying, 'If you love something, let it go free. If it returns, it is yours. If not, it never was.'"

I'd never thought of that before. I slept little that night. In the morning, I knew what I had to do. I asked one of my friends to see if Pablo wanted me to sign his hymnbook, as we often did at Bible Institute.

I was sitting on a bench in the auditorium before the afternoon class began when Pablo came up and asked me to sign his book. I wrote, "Pablo Mendez, if you love something, let it go free. If it returns, it is yours. If not, it never was. Susana Martin, November 1998."

* * *

That night after church, Pablo came to me and asked me if there was anything wrong. I said that he hadn't offended me and I hoped I hadn't offended him, but I didn't feel right in doing what my dad told me not to. I said that I felt guilty before God for what I had done.

He said he had too, and that it was just as much his fault as mine. We agreed to make things right with God's help.

Before I went to sleep that night, I made a pledge to God. "Lord, I know I've failed You in many ways, but, Lord, forgive me. I promise that with your help, I'll wait for Your good time in my life. Please remind me of this often..."

122

Doomed to Be Single?

READ: Philippians 4:11-13

As a young teen, I listened in astonishment when a friend stated that she thought twenty-one was a good age to start dating. "Twenty-one!" I groaned inwardly. "It's bad enough to wait until I'm eighteen. Twenty-one is old!"

Now as I remember that time in my life, I smile. At that age, having a boyfriend was very important to me. Then, as the years slipped by, I discovered that having a boyfriend wasn't the only important thing in life and that twenty-one wasn't old. I discovered that *single* isn't a bad word or a doomed lifestyle.

At times I still longed for a boyfriend, someone to love me. But I was free to go to Bible School, to become involved in mission work, and to make a difference in other people's lives. When I was content where God had placed me and involved in His work, I was happy and fulfilled. I still prayed that God would direct in my life and provide someone for me according to His will, but the desire for a companion didn't torment me day after day.

I look back over the past several years of service with satisfaction. I realize how much I would have missed had I married at a young age and how much joy I would have lost had I spent those years bemoaning my singleness.

If God has called you to be single longer than your friends (or even for life), don't fight God's will. Don't be a grouchy old maid. Serve God where He has placed you, and He will reward you with contentment.

Note: The writer is now happily married!

Seeing Love

READER: John 15:9-14

We all want to believe that life is good, right, just. Even the people who say life is meaningless wish it were not. We want to think that in the end the world does make sense. More than anything else, we ache for love.

Eventually, we meet reality. When we witness pain—extreme, relentless pain—it does not seem good. When we see innocent people—godly, kind-hearted people in anguish—it does not seem right. When we watch selfish people—greedy, heartless people going on undisturbed—it does not seem just. And when our own hearts lie oozing before us, it does not seem like love.

That is when we stop to see if the world is what we thought it was. That is when we wonder if the God in our bed-time stories was ever there.

I know a woman whose heart is aching, as it has been for sixty years. I know a faithful Christian who is daily tortured by another person's sins. I know a man who has long abused others, and is now the father of a helpless child.

And I am not very old. I have not seen much of life. There are pains more horrible than any I have felt. There are lives more tragic than any I have seen. There is enough injustice in the world to make me conclude that if there is a God, He is anything but love.

Still, I have caught a glimpse of a reality beyond the one that chokes me. I have caught a glimpse of Someone who created everything good, Someone who does everything right, Someone who is always just.

I have seen, outside the walls of a crowded city, a hill, and on that hill—a cross.

Love? Love.

And I marvel at a love so great that it can be seen in such a world.

by Sarah Yoder

(Used by permission, from: *The Calvary Messenger*)

What Makes It Love?

READ: Mark 12:28-33

Perhaps you, like me, have been thrilled to see two Christians placing their lives side by side in marriage. *What makes it love?* you wonder. Or maybe you've seen the wife ruining her morning's plans to run an errand for her hard-working husband. It's love, and it's beautiful!

But what makes it love? Isn't it the giving up of one's self?

I think about the words of Mark twelve: "Thou shalt love the Lord thy God with all thy heart, and with all thy soul, and with all thy mind, and with all thy strength." What a commitment! As I read that, my puny sacrifices shrivel like dried prunes.

I love the Lord. Or do I?

What is a love that will not sacrifice? What is a love that has not cried salty tears? What is a love that loses no sleep for its cause? What is a love that has not bruised its knees in prayer? What is a love that has not sacrificed wealth and popularity?

"Oh, God! A love is no love that will not suffer. Therefore, I commit myself to love You anew. Let it be a deep commitment, a commitment willing to

   bruise its knees,

     skin its knuckles,

       and be burned up for You!"

Be Mine

READ: Isaiah 43:1-7

They say "You're Sweet," "I'm Yours," "Say Yes," and "Be Mine." They appear in stores right after Christmas, and stay there until the Valentine's Day clearance sales are over. You know what they are—those candy hearts that people eat and pass out to their friends when February 14 rolls around.

Valentine's Day is a celebration of love. It's a time when people give sweet gifts in honor of the love they have for each other. Usually it celebrates romantic love, but what if you're single?

Being single is a blessing, even though I don't always look at it that way. Sometimes it can be lonely when it seems that everyone else is pairing up and finding love. Other girls are getting cards, flowers, and gifts, while I'm not receiving much.

But wait! God is sending me a message on Valentine's Day. It is a message straight from His heart, reflecting His undying love for me. He says, "Be Mine." He's telling me not to be envious of others, but to strive for a love that's lasting—His love. He's telling me to spend my time and energy on pursuing a close relationship with Him.

I am not alone, on Valentine's Day or any other day of the year. Jesus is always with me, encouraging me to be all I can be for Him. He gave His own heart to me, and now He says, "Be Mine."

In Love

READ: *Deuteronomy 6:3-5*

"Is he ever going to get off the phone?" we groaned as we stood in the living room. Looking at each other, we rolled our eyes.

Once again, my brother was talking on the phone with his out-of-state girlfriend. And, once again, he had a tough time keeping his conversation to less than an hour long.

"Think of the phone bill he'll have to pay," Mom remarked.

My brother didn't seem to mind the cost. He kept on talking.

When we exclaimed later about his phone bills, he only smiled. "We were just getting started good," he protested. "It's hard to believe we talked that long. When you're in love, you'll see what I mean."

I shook my head. "Don't you ever run out of things to say to each other?" I asked.

My brother laughed. I think he figured that getting any sympathy from me would be pretty hopeless.

Then, I realized that I had the opposite problem. I told Someone I loved Him, but didn't take time to talk with Him.

God was asking, "Do you truly love Me? You see what love does to your brother. Why can't it be that way with us? How can you say you love Me, but don't have time to be with Me? Our relationship is even more important than the kind of relationship your brother is building right now."

I cringed when I realized how little time I had actually spent alone with God, and how shallow my love was for Him. It was easy for me to think that I needed to pray because I **had** to please God, instead of praying because I loved Him and **wanted** to talk to Him.

God has taught me a lot about prayer since then. When I'm tempted to skimp on time with God, He comes back to me with a reminder. "Are you really 'in love' with Me?"

Chapter 9

Be Still, My Soul

Waiting to Serve

READ: Colossians 3:22-24

I wondered when God was going to answer my prayer. After all, I needed to decide what to do with my summer soon. I had to know how much money to raise and how to prepare for whatever I'd do. However, nothing seemed to open up for me. I wondered why waiting for God's will seemed so hard.

One evening I had to wash dishes. I started the task, although I wasn't very excited about it. I was merely enduring this little chore that was keeping me from doing more enjoyable things. As I watched the soap bubbles dance in the dishwater, I suddenly realized that I could be the Lord's servant if I did anything cheerfully. No matter how mundane the chore, I would be serving God right where I was.

When this thought sank in, I knew God had answered a part of my prayer. He was telling me that all I needed to do now was to live a normal life and be His servant while I was at home.

Waiting is a little easier to bear now, because I know that God will work out all the details for my plans. He knows my desires, He knows what's best for me, and He knows exactly when to bring everything together. God wants the best for His servants.

Kicking at Closed Doors

READ: John 10:7-9

The door was beautiful, no doubt about that. The Maker of the door had carved an amazing, intricate fashion on the priceless wood. I longed to open that beautiful door and discover the treasures beyond it.

I didn't know exactly what the door led to, but I had a good idea. I tried the doorknob. Locked! I approached the Maker confidently and stated, "I need a key."

He looked at me for a long time. Then, He turned His back and continued His work. I couldn't see the expression on His face when He answered, "I cannot give you the keys. You must wait until I open the right door. And, behind every door that I open, you will find happiness."

I headed back down the hallway of my life to the beautiful door. In my haste to reach it, I didn't stay to hear the Maker's next sentence. After the word *happiness*, I was sure that the Maker would swing the beautiful door open for me.

I waited for hours. Still, the Maker did not come. I traced the pattern on the door with tears streaming down my cheeks. How cruel the Maker was to make me wait so long.

I tried all the keys in my pocket. Every one was too small. I threw them to the floor and kicked the door impatiently. Still, it did not budge.

I sat down again. Perhaps the Maker's tender heart would melt when He saw my woebegone figure crouched before the beautiful door.

But more time passed, and still the Maker did not come. He had gone further away by this time. I could no longer hear

His cheery song as He went about His work.

I rose from the floor to find Him. Then, I saw it—an open door behind me. I could not see inside because it was only open a crack. But, oh, how ugly this door was! Blood streaked the rough wood. Surely this door could not lead to fulfillment.

I felt a hand on my shoulder, the hand of the Maker. "I will go through the door with you," He offered.

Grateful tears sprung to my eyes, for I was afraid of what lay on the other side of such an ugly door. I hesitated for a moment. Then, I remembered that the Maker had promised happiness. I knew that He did not lie, and I entered the door with Him.

I do not need to say what lay on the other side of the door. I only need to say that I found happiness, and I looked up into the Maker's loving face, promising that I would never kick at closed doors again.

"When God closes one door of happiness, He opens another. But often we look so long at the closed door that we do not see the one that has been opened for us."

Wait!

READ: Psalms 37:1-7

I sit impatiently waiting for a phone call. The public phone is being monopolized and I want to use it. Nevertheless, I have to wait. It's a part of life here in Guatemala.

I hurriedly get ready to go away. My co-worker says we will leave in five minutes. I wait an additional twenty minutes.

Waiting. Ouch! How I hate to wait. I think God is trying to teach me lessons on patience, but it is hard to sit still long enough to listen.

I've found that delays are a part of God's plan for my life. He uses these periods of waiting, whether they are five minutes or ten years, to develop character, to teach patience, to show who truly is in control, and to demonstrate His power.

When delays come, instead of wasting that time complaining, I can do something worthwhile:

1. Spend time praying.
2. Encourage a friend or witness to a neighbor who is also waiting.
3. Meditate on Scripture.
4. Write a letter.

If the waiting is long term, I need to serve God contentedly where He has placed me. Why not enjoy my present circumstances, instead of ruining that time in longing for the future?

Dear patient Heavenly Father, help me, an impatient-natured person, to learn the lessons You want to teach me. May I respond lovingly and patiently to the roadblocks and delays that you put in my path. Thanks for being patient with me. Amen.

Don't Peek

READ: Ecclesiastes 7:8-10

I scanned the living room hurriedly, looking for the perfect place to hide the thimble. In the next room, I could hear my brothers, anxiously shuffling and crowding to the door. Each one was eager to be the first one to find the thimble.

"Don't peek!" I warned as I stepped on the couch to set the thimble on the top window ledge. I pulled back. No, that would be too high for the younger ones to reach.

"Hurry up!" came someone's muffled voice. I knew of their impatience and that oh-so-strong temptation to peek. Quickly, I set the thimble behind a plant on the bookcase and yelled for them to come.

That curiosity streak to peek shows itself at birthday time, too. When I'm decorating the cake or smuggling gifts to the bedroom, I almost always have to caution, "Don't peek!"

"But why not?"

"Well, because you don't *have* to know what I'm doing or making. It's a surprise and I want it to be a secret until just the right moment. Can't you wait a little longer?"

How much like children we are when God is doing something in our lives that we can't see and understand! It seems we've *got* to know what His purpose is, why He's taking so long, why He won't let us peek.

However, like baby chicks that are protected by their mother, we are under His wings and covered with His feathers (Psalm 91:4). We don't need to peek out to see if He is keeping us safe! We don't need to peek out to see what is going on!

"But it is so dark," we whimper. "I can't see a thing. It is the blackest of nights."

Oh, Child, You have yet to understand. You are so close to His light that You can't see it. For there can never be a shadow unless there is light.

In His time, He will lift the wing, draw back the shadows, and reveal His plan. Until then, contentment under His feathers must be learned. Contentment in knowing that He has everything under control no matter how dark it seems.

We can be ever so happy and busy in accepting what God has for us now.

Just don't peek.

You'll Have to Wait

READ: Psalm 145:14-17

It's strawberry season again! Big, red, and juicy — what could taste better in the spring than fresh berries? Lift the leaves to find the cluster, however, and temptation will stare you in the face. You'll see a berry, still pink, but big enough to make your taste buds quiver. Will you pick it?

Take a moment to compare half-ripe strawberries with truly ripe ones. Light strawberries may reach great sizes, but they will usually swell if left to ripen. The color of a half-ripe strawberry may be a tempting pink, but a ripe one is startlingly red. A pink strawberry will have a distinct flavor. But how does a scarlet strawberry taste? It is tangy with spring's fresh air, juicy with its rain, and sweet as the sunshine!

Reason dictates that you pick only fully ripened strawberries. But you'll have to wait. It takes time for the sunshine and warm air to ripen them.

Other fruit requires time to ripen also. Perhaps you must be sixteen to get your driver's license. Seventeen to attend Bible school. Eighteen for courtship. Twenty for volunteer service in Guatemala. The fruit may be delicious, but you'll have to wait!

Maybe you're a little impatient with life. It seems like *right now* would be a good time to serve the Lord in volunteer service, teaching school, or serving in some other capacity. Your age or circumstances staunchly block the way. Don't despair! Those desires are like hard, white strawberries. In God's time and way they can ripen into juicy fruit, but you'll have to wait!

You *can* pick pink strawberries. You can even pick white strawberries if you want to. However, neither will be edible, and both will ruin the fruit's chance to ripen. You can try to rush life's circumstances if you want to. You can even throw guidelines away, taking on responsibilities and privileges before reaching the designated maturity. The consequences of doing this are like picking white berries. You'll ruin your chance for properly ripened, delicious fruit.

Scarlet strawberries are time ripened. And you'll have to wait.

Don't ruin tomorrow's fruit by picking it green today!

While You Wait

READch: Micah 6:6-9

Okay, you've decided that you will pick only ripe strawberries. Now you're faced with a dilemma. What should you do while waiting on those that are still half pink?

In the strawberry patch, you can squat on the straw and stare at the clusters, waiting for them to ripen. You can even turn them daily—the underside may ripen faster!

While waiting for God's fruit in your life, don't merely sit and stare. Neither should you rush the process. Search for other God-given opportunities.

God has a purpose for every year and every day of your life. He didn't give you a seventeenth year just to put in time until your eighteenth. He gave you a seventeenth year to serve Him in a unique way.

If you're longing to be a missionary, start preparing. Has your co-worker ever heard your testimony? Is your elderly neighbor lady a Christian? If you want to be a teacher, start collecting ideas. Work with children; develop your patience.

Whatever your desire, you can still serve God today. By helping in your home. By tackling your job with determination to glorify God. By influencing your friends in a positive way. By being a light to the world.

Don't overlook today's opportunities while you wait for tomorrow's strawberries!

The Package

READ: Matthew 6:25-34

Tonight
I bring You a package, Lord,
A package labeled FUTURE.
It's big,
    it's black, and Lord,
        it's heavy.

Sometimes
I notice rustlings,
    rattling,
        muffled thumps
From within the well-tied sides.
And worry, "What can they mean?"

This package, Lord,
I've dragged all day.
Now
The stars twinkle;
And I shudder to think
Of sleeping with it on my back.

"O God! Please take my burden.
It will not drop.
It must be anchored to my back
With thongs of my own weaving.
But Lord, You speak!
It will obey Your voice."

He speaks.

The bundle slides and drops
Beside Christ's feet. He stoops
And picks it up.

Then,
With gentle eyes,
And Father-love in His voice
He says,
    "My daughter,
    You could have asked at sunrise."

Keep on Fishing

READ: Habakkuk 2:1-4

I stared hard at the bobber on the end of my line. *Come on, fish. Bite!* I impatiently told the unseen salmon. I waited expectantly for the bobber to disappear, telling me that a fish was on my line.

The afternoon dragged on. Cast and pull in. Cast again. Every once in a while, salmon would leap out of the water, tantalizing me with their beauty. They wouldn't bite, though.

Just when I was beginning to wonder if anyone would catch any fish, one of the boys felt a tug on the end of his line. He handed the pole to me, and I had the opportunity of fighting the fish to shore. It was a new experience, battling a fish that weighed over twenty pounds. I gripped the pole with both hands, and braced myself.

A few minutes later the salmon lay on the sandbar. I looked at it with a sense of awe. That whole afternoon had been worth it, if even for that one fish. The waiting part suddenly wasn't so bad.

Then, God gently reminded me about some other things in my life. Sometimes I tend to get impatient. I want to know God's will right now. I don't want to wait for God to show me what to do. I keep wondering if waiting on God is really worth it.

Opportunities tantalize me, things I'd like to do right now. God says, "Not yet."

Sometimes I get tired of it. I'm tempted to quit fishing for God's will, when it seems like God isn't going to do anything about something that looks big and appealing to me.

That's when I need to remember the salmon. It was worth the wait. That afternoon, I knew that waiting on God would produce the greatest blessings I could ever hope to experience.

I'm going to keep on fishing!

The Applesauce Test

READ: Romans 8:23-28

"Oh, I should get some bologna out of the freezer for tomorrow's school lunches," I remembered. I opened the freezer door and...

"Crash!" A blue bowl sailed through the air. "Bang, boppity, bop!" Great waves of applesauce flung in every direction and coated everything in sight.

"The test of a true woman," flashed through my mind. I bit my lip. I didn't dare say anything; if I did, it certainly wouldn't be edifying. I wasn't at all amused at the rivers of applesauce dribbling down the windows and cupboards.

Gritting my teeth, I grabbed a rag and set to work. As my rag sucked up giant pools and splatters of sticky yellow goo, a wry grin tugged at my lips. I mulled over that phrase, "the test of a true woman."

Applesauce often "flies out of the freezer" in other ways. When my day is planned, and I find out at the last minute that someone else has totally different plans for me, it's like an applesauce bath. Yuck. I have to ask God to keep me from getting impatient.

Inevitably, I encounter pain, and it's as if God threw applesauce all over my life. The smallest incidents eject giant waves, and even after I think I've cleaned it up, I find hidden splatters here and there. It's the test of a true woman.

Often, I have no idea what the future holds. Things may be going well, when out of nowhere, a bowl sails through the air and messes up my life. Sigh.

Every time I encounter the "test of a true woman," the applesauce test, I have to be patient, and ask God to come with His rag and clean me up.

Be Still, My Soul

READ: Psalm 46

Be still my soul; the Lord is on thy side. Bear patiently the cross of grief or pain.

This song became "mine" the year our family moved out of state. I sang it in times of quiet devotion with tears running down my cheeks. It calmed my heart. The pain of leaving friends and church family was sharp, but God's love was still there.

Leave to thy God to order and provide. In every change He faithful will remain.

So then, why do I so often want to order and provide? Why does it become difficult to trust in God to do what He has promised to do? He would continue to be faithful in each change I was going through—new community, new church, new friends.

Be still my soul: thy best, thy heavenly Friend...through thorny ways leads to a joyful end.

Even here on earth, God has joyous things in store for me. I found out in the months that followed. Life in the new land was joyously exciting and many new things came my way.

When disappointment, grief, and fear are gone. Sorrow forgot, love's purest joys restored.

Heaven will be worth it all. Joy, in the fullest sense, will be restored.

Be still my soul: when change and tears are past, all safe and blessed we shall meet at last.

Change, here on earth, is inevitable. But listen, Soul! In heaven I will be safe and blessed forever and ever! I want to be ready for the final move.

How often in the busyness of the day, when worries swirl to dizzying heights and the pressure is on, I hear God say, "Be still and know that I am God." When there's so much to do, I just need to remind myself, "Be still, my soul! Just stop for a minute and remember that God is GOD. He will always BE God."

I feel so insignificant before Him, but He cares for me as an individual. He cared so much that He died for me. So, be still, my soul!

Will my soul listen? Will I take my eyes off the storm and look to the Calmer of the waves? Will I take my eyes off my sin and look to the Savior? Will I take my eyes off my grief and look to the Healer? Be still my soul!

Amen.

The Big Deal About Change

READ: Malachi 3:1-6

"No!" I wanted to scream to the whole world. "I don't want to leave!" As I sat in a folding chair at school, I felt sick. Yes, I was a bit sick. I still had my cold. But, I also felt sick at heart. I did not want to finish ninth grade. And I could do nothing about it. Soon, I would leave school, this time for good. After that, I would have to study at home.

Why? Why doesn't our school have more than ninth grade? my mind asked. I could not answer that question. I just knew that soon, too soon, I would say goodbye to my classmates.

I was excited at the same time. Interesting things were happening and would continue to happen. But in my mind I could see days ahead when I would wish to return to my dear old school.

After our class sang a song, we received our ninth grade diplomas. It felt very special, being with my classmates this final time receiving our diplomas. They even had to nudge me to go when we were done. I was in a daze.

Cameras flashed all around us later, as we posed for pictures. My classmates and I shook each other's hands. It was fun and at the same time, I realized that this was over. I would soon go home, and I wouldn't see some of my friends very often after that night.

Have you ever thanked God for being changeless? Well, I did. I had finally realized how beautiful that was. Before, I could never understand what the big deal was about Him being changeless. Now I do.

Although my circumstances may change, His love for

me is still the same. Even when I go through painful changes, God will always care about me. His comforting presence and compassion never change.

"Thank You so much, God, for being changeless. You are the same yesterday, today, and tomorrow. I love You for not changing!"

Growing Up

READ: 1 Samuel 20:1-17

Changing is a part of growing up. Over the last few years, my friends, my circumstances, and myself have changed. Sometimes it was easy to adjust, but other times it was really hard. One of the most confusing changes has been a change in my friendships.

I have a kindred spirit that I've known for years. We've always been able to talk with each other for hours, about everything. But our friendship changes as we grow and get to know more people. When this first began, I was confused and a little upset. Why couldn't things always be like they used to be? Now we could never be alone together, because other good friends were always with us. I even began to question whether she still thought of me as a kindred spirit, or if she didn't need me in her life anymore.

One evening when we were talking on the phone, she tactfully said, "Sherilyn, you seem different sometimes. Does it bother you that we have other friends and hardly get a chance to be alone together?"

I admitted that, yes, it did. I said that I wished things could be just like they were, before we...well, before we started to grow up.

She then assured me of her friendship and encouraged me to think of our relationship as a "kindred spirit" relationship, not a "best friend" one. Kindred spirits always have room for others. Best friends might grow apart and get new best friends, but kindred spirits are forever.

That encouraging conversation was just what I needed to hear. I learned that we have to be open and honest with each other to keep our friendship on the right track.

The Bible tells about some close friends. Take David and Jonathan or Ruth and Naomi for example. You can read about them to find out how they dealt with change, and how they stayed close through it all.

I'm learning that it's up to me to decide how to deal with changes in my friendships. I can resist every new circumstance. Or, I can face changes head-on with God's help. I'm sure that will make a difference.

Chapter 10

We Rest on Thee

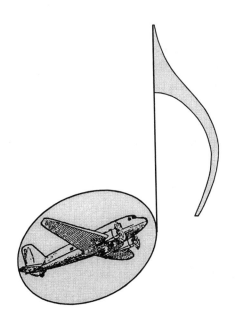

Replacing Fears

READ: Isaiah 12

The very thought of giving a speech in front of a group of people terrifies me. No matter how hard I try to squelch my nervousness, it still hits me full force when I'm trying to gather my thoughts into clear words. I'm even frightened by the thought of giving a short testimony.

I wish speeches were the only thing I'm afraid of. Unfortunately, I seem to meet up with scary situations a lot. Witnessing, apologizing, big groups of people, and even youth group activities scare me sometimes.

Although I often remind myself that I'm an adult, not a child anymore, I still can't relieve my own fears. God is the only One who understands everything I face, and He has all the answers I need. Isaiah 12:2 contains the sentence, "I will trust, and not be afraid." These words have helped me tremendously when I needed courage. When I say the verse over and over, God helps me to be calm and to face the things I'm afraid of.

The Bible also says that God cares about the sparrow when He sees it fall. When I think about that, I know that He cares about everything I face. He can replace my fears with confidence.

It Is I

READ: Psalm 107:28-31

The wind is howling furiously,
and my boat is surging
through the clammy mist.
Tears
mingle with salty spray
and stream down my face
as I clutch my frail skiff
that drifts ever closer to the rocks.
Choked,
as the mist tightens, I hear the ocean
slapping viciously against the shore.
Icy water hurls itself upon sharp cliffs,
a cruel, crawling foam that threatens
to wreck my ship upon the reefs!
I am crying
and shaking with fear.
Then,
I hear a voice amidst the storm.
I strain to listen…
It is calling…calling…
It is Jesus
saying,
"My Child,
it is I.
Do not be afraid.

What If?

READ: *Numbers 14:1-9*

Children have many fears. Some fear "boogie men" under the bed or bears waiting to grab them in the dark. When I was a child, bears and "boogie men" paled in comparison to airplanes.

Airplanes were noisy monsters. I could hear them growling overhead while I played in the yard. They were big. What if an airplane crashed on top of me? Or, what if one dropped on our house? My vivid imagination pictured the destruction.

My parents told me to trust God, but that did not satisfy me. Airplanes *did* crash sometimes, and one *might* crash on me. Whenever a jet flew overhead, I clung to my mother's skirt until the danger passed. I needed her presence.

I'm not sure when my fear of airplanes changed to enjoyment. Now, I can't imagine being afraid of airplanes. I feel as safe on them as I do on the ground. I love the rumble of jets taking off and landing.

No, I'm not afraid of airplanes anymore. I fear other things, smaller than airplanes, but just as big in my mind.

There's the fear of what others think of me. I wonder, *Do they think I'm boring? What if they don't like me? What will they think if I...*

Or I struggle with fears about the future. My thoughts churn, *What if God leads me to a place or situation I can't handle? What if I would marry the wrong person? What if...*

My childhood fears look petty. "But the fears I'm facing now are *real*," I tell God.

"Are they?" He probes. "Does what people think matter

150

more than what I think? Would I allow something in your life you couldn't handle or that isn't my will for you?"

I face my motley and bedraggled array of "what if's." I hide my face in my hands. "Lord, why can't I overcome these fears?" I cry. "What if I never become what You want me to be?"

I huddle in embarrassment. Another "what if" has jumped into my bag of fears.

God doesn't scold. He assures me, "I am here, Child. Trust Me."

The "what if's" dissolve. I am safe in my Father's presence.

Imagine That!

READ: 2 Corinthians 10:3-5; 1 Chronicles 28:9

My imagination works hard...

"Why didn't she sit beside me? There's an empty chair. Is she ashamed to be my friend?"

"What does that fellow think of me? He might be watching me, and he even said 'hello' to me when he walked in!"

"What if I'm weird, but no one ever told me? Maybe my youth group can't stand me."

My imagination sends me on a torturous Ferris wheel of worry. (I imagine yours can, too.) Then Isaiah 26:3 flashes at me. "Thou wilt keep him in perfect peace whose [imagination] is stayed on thee: because he trusteth in thee." (My center-column reference substitutes *imagination* for *mind*.) The Lord must have inspired that verse for girls like me.

"Forgive me, Lord," I pray. "My focus has shifted to myself and what others think of me. Let me look up at You. Keep my imagination in check as I marvel at Your greatness."

What a wonder! My worry dissolves as I focus on Him. He understands the imagination that leaves me puzzled and exhausted. He's the ultimate Understander. Imagine that!

His Way Is Perfect

READ: Deuteronomy 32:1-4

"As for the Lord, HIS way is perfect: the word of the Lord is tried: He is a buckler to all those that trust in Him" (Psalm 18:30).

Sometimes we human beings like to look around at other ways, others paths to follow. We think:

"This passage surely wasn't meant for today. Clearly it was directed to just the church at that time."

As for the Lord, His way is perfect...

"I see nothing wrong in going to a fortune teller. That way I would know the future so I could follow God's will."

As for the Lord, His way is perfect...

"God *can't* be calling me there! He knows how much I would detest the heat and bugs. With the abilities He's given me, I'm sure He'd want me to take this office job."

As for the Lord, His way is perfect...

"How could my parents forbid me to date him? They don't even *know* him. I'm sure God is leading us together."

As for the Lord, His way is perfect...

I don't think we yet understand that God's way IS PERFECT or else we would have learned by now to quit trying our own methods and the devil's ways.

Not only is His way absolutely flawless, completely accurate, and exactly excellent; but it has been tried, proven, and tested by thousands before us. They *knew* it worked, they *proved* it worked, and they're waiting for the rest of us who have done the same to join them in heaven.

As perfect as God's way is, it can also be lonely. So few people choose that narrow path. Then He becomes our Buckler, our Protection, our Defense. He will never leave us. He was with us even before we knew it.

When we begin to follow His perfect way, we realize how imperfect our own way is. As He cleanses us, we can shout victoriously: "It is God that girdeth me with strength and maketh my way (*what else?*) PERFECT" (Psalm 18:32).

The Cling of Trust

READF: Jeremiah 17:5-8

When I was a preschooler, our family went to the cabin. I well remember the swing. It was no ordinary swing, but merely a board knotted to the end of a bristled rope. Dangling from a tree limb, it hung above the brow of a hill. To my childish eyes, it looked awfully high.

I still remember Daddy balancing me on the board. Then he pushed me, and I soared above the slope. My heart surged with excitement and fear. Would the board drop off? Would I never reach the zenith and return? I clung to the rope because there was nothing else within reach.

Years have passed since that swing ride. Yet, I'm sitting again on the board of another swing. The foggy future slopes before me. Uncertainty and challenge pound within my heart. I feel the shove that sends me soaring. My heart panics, "Where will this end, Lord? Will we never come back to familiar ground?" Finding nothing trustworthy but Him, I cling to His strength.

The swing ride I experienced years ago ended safely. I even learned to enjoy the exhilaration enough to ride several more times before leaving.

Today, I'm beginning to enjoy the uncertainty that makes me trust. Leery and unprepared, I swing into the future. I cling to God. And always, He brings me back to familiar ground and rest in Him.

God is my rope. He knows that fear is not the only emotion prompting my fingers to grip until they're white. It is the cling of trust.

He's Everything to Me

READ: Hebrews 13:5-8

Sometimes our world gets a little topsy-turvy. We realize we can't trust totally in people and things. They fail. That's when our search begins for Someone who can be everything to us.

> Friends will come and friends will go,
> There's so many folks I know.
> But there's a friend who'll never flee,
> He's everything to me.

> Safe within His tender care,
> I can rest, knowing *He is there.*
> Although the way I cannot see.
> I know He's always there for me.

> His love for me will never dim,
> Forever I'll belong to Him.
> He comforts, gladdens, and makes free,
> My King is everything

Learning Faith

READD: Hebrews 11:1-6

I thought I had faith
    'Til a towering thunderhead
    smothered the sun.
Then I learned that God is still God
    Without the sunshine;
        And I thanked Him for light.

I thought I had faith
    Until dark followed dusk with
    an obstinate blind.
Then I learned that God is still God
    Without the light;
        And I thanked Him for the moon.

I thought I had faith
    'Til a cloud masked the
    moon's silver light.
Then I learned that God is still God
    Without the moon;
        And I thanked Him for stars.

I thought I had faith
    Until even the stars melted
    into the storm.
Then I learned that faith
    Is believing God is God

When there is
nothing left
but
Him.

And then I realized that
He
is
everything.

Hope and a Future

READ: Jeremiah 29:10-14

An outcast—someone who hurts because he's a leftover, a loser. Many people feel like this all the time, and I suppose everybody has felt it at one time or another. Can we be delivered from this hopeless feeling?

When I was in the seventh and eighth grades, I became painfully aware of how unkind people could be to each other. By saying things behind other people's backs or not including them in a conversation, they sent clear messages that not everyone was as good as they were. I often wondered why we couldn't all get along and strive to make life easier for our friends and classmates. We were only interested in putting other people down and making ourselves look better.

The summer before ninth grade, there was a revival in the community. A lot of us either became Christians or made a recommitment during that time. As ninth grade began, everyone made a real effort to be the kind of person God wanted them to be.

The difference was amazing. Cliques dissolved, and everyone had a kind word to say. God had given the former outcasts hope!

One of my favorite songs is based on Jeremiah 29:11. The verses talk about being discouraged and asking God for help. The chorus is God's reply:

"For I know the plans that I have for you,
Plans to give you hope,
Plans to give you courage
When the pressures are too much;
Plans not to harm you
But to prosper you today;
Oh, my Child, trust in Me,
I will show you the way."*

It is comforting to know that if I obey God and trust Him, He will give me hope—and a bright future.

*Rose Troyer, 1992
Used by permission

Believe It or Not!

READ: Matthew 8:23-27

Just think! When a chicken lays an egg, the egg falls on the side where the shell is harder to protect the embryo inside. When it's time for the chick to enter the world, he pecks on the soft side of the egg where it's easier to come out. That's one of the wonders of God's creation.

Do you understand how the ocean waves work in relation to the moon? I never quite get it. I only know that somehow the gravity of the moon pulls on the ocean tide, forming waves. Who planned it that way?

Atoms are everywhere—in the air, in chemicals and in plants. Billions of them are in you. Look around. Everything you see has atoms so small that you can't see them with even a powerful microscope. Who made such tiny little things and understands how they all work?

God!

Why can't I trust God, the One who knows it all, the One who made it all? If He is in control over nature, He is in control over my life too. I just need to learn to trust Him.

Myself?

READ: 2 Corinthians 5:14-17

"**W**ho is myself?" I ask in desperation. "How can I be myself if I don't know who myself *is*?" The mysterious thing that I call "myself" seems to change so vulnerably and incomprehensibly.

Last night after church, when I was jabbering away to my girlfriends, I was an extrovert, right? Okay, so here I am, wearing the extrovert hat. Jocularly I step into a group of strangers and...oops. My extrovert hat has disappeared completely! In its place sits an uncomfortable introvert cap. I manage a timid "hi," and slip away. Down the hall I meet a good friend, and wow! My extrovert hat pops on. Another friend joins us, and strangely, the introvert squeezes my head again.

What's wrong with me? Feeling alarmed and inferior, I crawl into a corner and vow to stop wearing hats forever.

I soon discover that extremist methods don't work. Without anything on my head, I get cold, wet, and bruised in stormy weather. Furthermore, I feel even more self-conscious because everyone else seems to be wearing a hat.

In desperation, I go to the closet to search for a new hat. There I find a sturdy, durable hat labeled "Jesus Christ." Hmmm...I need to try this.

To my surprise and pleasure, it fits perfectly! Inexplicable things begin happening. When I am chattering nonstop at a girl's party, I suddenly think of the hat I am wearing, and check my words. In a group of strangers, this new hat of Jesus gives me courage and stability. What's more, it stays on in any situation or weather!

The key to unlocking myself lies not in discerning and balancing my temperament. Temperaments change. The key is in the Changeless One. When Jesus Christ fills my life with His presence, I find myself secure and restful.

Myself?

Not I, but Christ in me. Christ is my all in all.

Chapter 11

Into our Hands

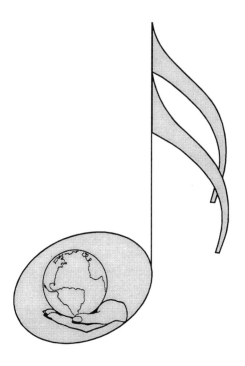

Service

READ: Matthew 25:34-46

God, I feel so discouraged tonight! As I tiredly washed stacks of dirty dishes, my tears dripped into the sudsy water. *Dishes, laundry, cleaning...is this all You want me to do? I feel so mundane in this never-ending cycle of WORK. I wash, weed, and sweep, only to do everything all over again! I am busy from early in the morning until late at night, but I have nothing to show for it. That is, nothing but chapped hands, weary feet, and an exhausted body and mind! Oh God, what am I doing for You?*

"My child, take heart. My plan for you right now is fulfilled when you are cheerfully caring for your family, folding laundry, doing dishes, and weeding the garden. The clean, smiling faces that go to school, the rows of canned vegetables, and the loaves of bread on the counter serve as witnesses of your love for Me. Whether you are sewing buttons or grading papers for your dad, you are serving Me. When you read Bible stories to your brothers and sisters, help them with their homework, or play Memory with them, you are My missionary. You praise Me every day by your frequent prayers, your cheerful song, and your unselfish service. These things are, to Me, the greatest kind of worship."

Dirty Hands and Watered Hearts

READ: 1 Corinthians 3:6-9

Today I worked in my new garden. What a joy to feel the moist, black soil in my hands! It felt so good to crumble the dirt around my rose bush.

As I sat there, pulling out the weeds, I asked myself just how much I enjoy working in the corner where God put me. Do I love making friends and preparing the soil of their hearts? How much time do I spend with other people, telling them about a Savior that wants to make beautiful things out of their lives?

After I finished working up the ground, I watered my plants. I could imagine the thirsty plants just drinking it up after being in the heat of El Salvador all day. The ground seemed to take it all in and then ask for more. It didn't matter if I got all wet, just so my plants would grow and be fruitful someday.

Do I go to the bother of giving myself so others can be refreshed with a little note, a kind word, or even only a smile? In this world, many people are hurting and need a little love. Do I shrug them off and go on with my own business?

I can hardly wait to see what my garden will look like when it's done. Red roses, colorful zinnias, juicy grapes and elephant ears will make a beautiful picture. But what would happen if I wouldn't sprinkle a bit of water on it for about a week? (I hope I won't forget!) Slowly, the plants would dry up. How sad that would be after all the work I put in it!

Am I keeping my other garden moist for my plants, so they can be refreshed and grow? Or am I too lazy to help them? If I persevere in watering their lives, my friends will be able to grow into beautiful plants. Their flowers will be a beauty in God's garden.

Once a Seed

READ: Mark 4:30-32

We cluster on the sidewalks,
    our little group,
        with hands full of tracts,
        with smiles on our faces.
Somehow, I feel as if we're carrying
    in our cupped hands
    measures of mustard seeds—
To be flung into the wind
        one…by…one.
Where will they fall?
        God alone knows.

Can it be?
        Just a glance,
            a greeting,
                and a paper tract—
Merely three seconds to live the Gospel

in front of curious passerby.
What tiny mustard seeds!

I drop a little seed
     Into a stranger's hand (and heart?),

     and pause.

Can it be that the Kingdom of God
     will sprout out of
        these?

And then I remember:
     A mustard seed, within God's hand,
     can grow into a mustard tree;

And every mustard tree
     was
        once
           a seed.

"Although your opportunities may be small,
never underestimate their potential!"

After the Harvest

READ: John 4:34-36

Faster and faster my hands moved, searching the luscious plants, grasping the berries. *Plink, plink, plink,* a red stream of strawberries dropped into the box, filling box after box, tray after tray...

Mosquitoes hovered in the blistering heat, darting in to satisfy their bloody thirst on my warm, damp skin. Rash crept up my arms and legs, leaving itching, watering bumps. Sunburn flamed over my face, yet I could not cease the work.

Work, work, work. My body was weary, my feet leaden, my back aching; still, I forced myself to work ever faster. The harvest was abundant and urgent. But I had a goal. After hours of labor, I would reach the end of the row. And at the end—there was rest.

Faster and faster my hands must work, searching the souls around me. Abundant needs are cropping up, people that are hungry and thirsty for God. More and more are trying to find Him, more and more are ready to hear the Gospel...

Feelings of inadequacy dart in, robbing me of strength and vitality. Discouragement threatens to dissolve my courage, abolish my faith. I am overwhelmed with the daily load of work, and I cry to God for relief.

Work, work, work. My mind is weary, my hands are worn, my body is tired; still, I must ask God to help me work ever faster. The message is urgent, the harvest abundant, the time limited. But I have a goal. After perhaps years of labor, I will reach the end of my life. At the end awaits heaven. And in heaven, there is rest.

Into My Hands?

READ: *2 Corinthians 5:18-21*

I'd like to know why I always get this lump in my throat whenever we sing song #209 in the *Christian Hymnal*. I guess it steps on my toes and makes me feel pretty inadequate at the same time.

We sang it again tonight. "Into our hands the Gospel is given..." Lord, it's not talking about *my* hands, is it? Not after what happened at the orthodontist's office Thursday.

I had a new nurse (or whatever you call an orthodontist's assistant). I'm always suspicious of new ones, because I hate the feel of inexperienced hands in my mouth.

She started poking this wire around in my mouth: pulling it out, measuring again, and sticking it back in. It hurt, but I didn't want to make her feel bad, so I suffered in silence.

I'm not sure what she was doing when she asked me what church I went to, but whatever it was, it HURT. I thought to myself, *Lady with the red hair, I'm more interested in the question of where you learned to do this wire stuff.*

So I said shortly, "Ozark Mennonite."

"Oh, neat," she said. Then she didn't say anything for a long time. That "golden moment" we keep singing about.

Okay, Lord, I have no excuses. I know it was rotten of me to keep silent just because my teeth hurt. We could have gotten into an interesting discussion, because I know she was curious. She must have been bursting with questions to ask.

So what's the deal with committing the Gospel into *my* hands, Lord? I ask You for opportunities. Then, when they come along, something as trivial as hurting teeth keep me from using those golden moments. I am so ashamed of myself, Lord.

I love You a lot, but if You're looking for someone to carry Your precious message, You'd better search somewhere else.

And yet...I don't want to sit idle while millions go to hell. I really don't have a choice in this, do I? Time is passing swiftly, and I want to reap glory, not tears.

All right, God, You've given the Gospel into my hands. Since my hands have been so useless lately, I confess this sin of neglect. (To her that knoweth to do good, and doeth it not, to her it is sin.) I offer You my hands, and my mouth too! You take and use them, because I can't. Also, would You give me another chance to witness to "Miss Red-Head?"

Lord, I still can't sing "Into Our Hands" without a lot of eye moisture. But, perhaps we should sing it more often. That way, I won't forget my promise to You.

A Crazy Missionary?

READ: Luke 9:57-10:3

"You're going to Guatemala?! You're crazy!" exclaimed one of my coworkers, when she found out about my plans.

"Isn't there a lot of violence in that country?" asked another one.

Some responded with more encouragement. "That's great." "I admire you."

I quit my good job to work on V.S. wages. I left family and friends. I went to a country with a different culture and a new language. But I knew God had called me to go and He would help me through the adjustments.

When I reflect on the past several years in Guatemala, I know that it wasn't a crazy thing to do. It has been a learning and growing experience, and I have been blessed in the process.

Did I face discouragements, homesickness, failures, and times of weakness? Yes. Being a missionary doesn't make me perfect. But when I am willing to serve God, He encourages me and works through me in spite of my imperfections.

Did I have to be extra talented to become a missionary? By all means, no! God uses anyone who is willing.

What have been some of the rewards of my time spent in missionary service? Understanding the Spanish language. Building relationships with the young girls in the church and helping them spiritually. Seeing changed lives and marveling at the power of prayer. Meeting people's health needs through my work in the clinic. Realizing that joy doesn't come through the possessions I have, but through my service to the Lord.

When I see all the work that is yet to be done on the mission field and the lack of workers, it saddens me. My prayer is that those whom God is calling to mission work will be willing to follow His leading.

These Are Your Hands

READ: 2 Corinthians 12:9-11

Now that I've given my life to God, what if He asks me to do something that I don't want to do?

Have you ever thought that? After all, it has happened many times in Christian history.

I read of the martyrs of the New Testament. Those that made the Hall of Faith in Hebrews 11 endured things they didn't exactly volunteer to do. As I read the list of their sufferings, my Americanized mind could not begin to grasp what they had to go through.

Then there are those a little closer to my time period. Those who gave of themselves because it was what God asked of them. Those who gave because there was nothing else to do but give. I read in a mission newsletter of the famine in North Korea. Tuberculosis was rampant. Hospitals were under-equipped and understaffed. Amid the heartache there were those who gave, *literally* gave, of themselves. A nurse, who did not have proper suction equipment to suction mucus from a TB patient's lungs, used her own mouth.

Then there was the story I heard a woman tell when I was younger. While in a concentration camp, the guards took her to a room that she was to clean. She stared at the room in horror. The floor was covered with human excrement and there was nothing to remove it with. She would have to use her own hands.

The guards left her and she struggled with mental torment.

Not doing it meant torture and death; to do it would be impossible. She looked at her hands. They were *her* hands, after all. To use them as a shovel for all the filth…

She struggled there for several moments until, at last, peaceful tears streamed down her cheeks. "These are not my hands, Lord," she whispered. "These are Your hands."

I like to think that perhaps that is the same prayer the nurse in North Korea prayed when she bent over the TB patient. The impossible became possible when given to the Lord. The same with the martyr at the Roman stake: "I offer my body to You, Lord, as a living sacrifice…"

The same with you and me, too. It is so easy to whimper, "Why?" God wants us to change that *Y* to a *Yes*. Only when we give in will He enable.

The task is to clean up the floor after a sick sibling. "These are Your hands, Lord. I do this for You."

The letter you've been putting off because you know it will not be easy to write. "These are Your hands, Lord. I do this for You."

God asks you to witness for Him to someone you never thought you could. "My mouth is Yours, Lord. I do this for You."

Faith: it's more than knowing that He *can*, it's knowing that He *will*.

Liberty!

READ: 1 Peter 1:18-21

Today is September 15, El Salvador's Independence Day. People make a big fuss over it. Businesses, stores, and schools are closed. Bands play as parades march down the streets. But what impresses me most is the "antorchas," the liberty torches.

Join me by the side of the road to see one go by. Okay, here they come. Sirens wail, trucks blow their horns and people cheer. Flags flap against a crowded bus. Happy people wave at us. Now a man comes running with a burning torch. Another man runs beside him. Huffing and puffing, they trot by. Two more men come behind stretching a big El Salvadoran flag. Police trucks follow. The officers smile as they slowly go by. Other trucks bring up the rear and the "antorcha" procession is gone.

You ask what the torch means. According to what I've heard, it's a reminder of when the declaration of independence was signed in Guatemala City in 1821. Messengers ran to El Salvador bearing the news of the independence of Central America. That's what the torch means—the message of liberty.

Liberty! What does the word liberty mean to us? Do we only remember the freedom of our country or do we also remember when we were slaves to Satan? Satan was a cruel master, but Jesus paid a real sacrifice so we could be free. Does this tug at our hearts or have we heard it so often we get tired of it?

We are called to be his messengers. We must go announce to others that we are free now. Is this exciting, or are we too tired to run? Jesus did the biggest job—dying for us on the cross. We need to tell others.

Let's run with the torch!

Do I Have Time?

READ: Luke 10:25-37

We had gone to an all-day meeting and were finally headed for home, two hours away. After traveling for an hour and a half, we met a stranded vehicle pushed to the side of the road. People milled around the vehicle, working to fix the truck.

Surely there are enough people here that we don't need to stop, I thought.

Much to my dismay, we stopped to help them. Didn't our driver realize that we were tired and wanted to get home? Evidently, he was much more compassionate than I was.

Five minutes passed. Eight minutes. Then ten minutes.

"God, I need an extra dose of patience right now," I prayed.

Finally, after fifteen minutes, we were on our way again, leaving behind a fixed truck and some grateful people.

Do I take the time to stop and help people whom I meet? It may be an old lady with her arms full of groceries who needs help. Or, it could be my younger brother who wants me to tie his shoes *now*, just when I happen to be busy kneading bread. Am I willing to take the time to wash my hands, bend down, and tie his shoes?

As a student in school, suppose I decide to stay in at recess to catch up with my work? What is my response when a younger student chatters incessantly or wants help with his work? Do I have time for him?

"Our time should always be viewed in light of eternity."

Chapter 12

Channels Only

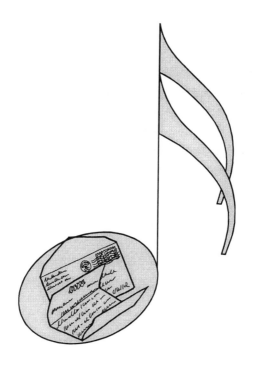

With an Empty Basket

READ: Exodus 3:1-14; 4:10-12

Baskets of apples. Baskets of Indian corn. Baskets of squash. Earth's harvest fills them all.

Lord, what can You do with an empty basket? I wish for something worthwhile to bring You, but I can't find even a kernel. I once thought I had talents, but when I glimpse Your greatness, they wither. Lord, I'm just—just an empty basket.

My writing talent is limited. You see how I struggle to write simply. And You've asked me to write for a book?

Teaching talent? Haven't You noticed my failures while substituting? How could You use a teacher like me?

I know, Lord, that I'm needed in the daily housework. Yet even there I make many mistakes, burning rolls and putting clean wash in the wrong drawers. Talent? Hardly.

I wish I had something to bring You, Father. You could use a basket of special talents, but I come painfully empty. What can You do with an empty basket?

My daughter, you do not understand. Empty baskets are the only ones that can overflow with My presence. They alone can go in My strength. My daughter, empty baskets are the few that I can fill.

A Nail and a Promise

READ: Matthew 25:14-30

When I saw the Guatemalan stamp, it didn't take long to tear the letter open. I devoured every word. The letter was typical of my friend who was teaching school in Guatemala. Even her handwriting looked busy.

I put the letter down. For a moment, I had been bouncing to the hospital with a van full of injured people. I could almost see the glow in the Indian childrens' eyes when my friend read the Christmas story. The image soon faded as the reality of where I was flooded back again.

I was in the States, looking through the window at the dreary landscape and thinking, *She's serving the Lord in Guatemala while it seems like I do nothing here in the States. What have I done for the Lord?* The trees outside looked cold and bare. "Nothing," they seemed to answer my thoughts.

Doubts began to appear. They peeked in the windows of my heart crying, "You must not mean a lot to God if He doesn't let you do anything for Him." I hesitated. The doubts clamored for entrance. I cracked the door and stared them in the face. They tried to reason their way into my soul.

On an impulse, I pulled a box of letters down from my closet. I picked out a fat envelope with a Guatemalan stamp, pulled a letter out, and scanned it. Suddenly, I slammed the door on the army of doubts when a sentence jumped out at me. "Thanks also for the insight on 'a nail'—it beautifully met the moment's need and is still in the process of encouraging me when I feel small and inadequate," my friend had written.

What was that about? I wondered. Then, I remembered.

An obscure verse in the book of Ezra had challenged me, and I had shared that challenge in one of my letters. I could not remember exactly what the thought had been. My friend remembered, however, and was encouraged by it.

The doubts drifted away, seeking someone else to plague. God was saying to me, "He (or she!) that is faithful in that which is least is faithful also in much." I wasn't at the front of the battle, but I had given a little boost to someone who was. Wasn't that just as important in God's sight? I thought of a song that perfectly expressed what I was thinking.

"It may not be on the mountain's height,
Or over the stormy sea;
It may not be at the battle's front
My Lord will have need of me;
But if by a still, small voice He calls
To paths that I do not know,
I'll answer, dear Lord, with my hand in Thine,
I'll go where You want me to go."

My heart thrilled to the promise in that song. "Ok, Lord," I said. "What's the next 'little' job You have for me?"

Sharing Sorrows

READ: Galatians 6:2-10

She sat across the table from me as we waited for our pizza, dabbing at the tears on her cheeks. What could I say? What could I do to heal the pain in her heart?

She was the manager of the place where I used to work. Even though she was probably in her mid-fifties, we had become good friends. We talked a lot about God.

I didn't know much about her background. I knew that she no longer lived with her abusive husband. And, as she told me her struggles that day, I knew that she was scared of him.

What was there to say? What could I, a young woman, possibly do to encourage? I felt I had no advice to give. I could do nothing but pray. So, when the pizza came, I added a special blessing just for her.

Was it enough? When we parted a while later, I gave her a big hug and tried to say something that would linger in her memory, to give her hope.

Was it enough? It seems like I should have done something more. I should have quoted some Scripture promises and encouraged her to keep following Jesus. I should have let her pain go more deeply into my heart and shed tears along with her. Did I really do enough?

As a Christian, I know I am placed on earth to encourage. I can point people to the God of all comfort and the Father of mercies. He is the only one who truly understands the language of tears.

My prayer today is that I will never be so caught up in the minor discomforts of my life that I would overlook another's deep pain. Someone has to be there for them. After all, someone was there for me.

You Can Do It!

READ: Philippians 1:2-8

Never underestimate the power of an encouraging word!

Recently, my nine-year-old brother incorporated a new slogan into our vocabulary. I'm not exactly sure of the situation where it was first used, but I do remember when he first used it on me.

I was toying with the food on my plate, feeling too full to finish and a little embarrassed for not cleaning my plate off. My brother eyed me with a mischievous twinkle in his eye.

"Come on! You can do it! You can do it!"

I laughed helplessly. It was so ironic—a little brother encouraging his big sister to clean off her plate. I did finish it, thanks to his chipper words, "You can do it!"

My family knows now that to make me laugh, all they have to say is that simple aphorism. My brothers have slightly abused it, though. When they beg me to do something for them, they end with, "You can do it! Come on, you can do it!"

We will go through our lives either being a blessing or a curse to other people. We need to recognize the high value of other people and the importance of small encouragements. Our lives are made up of a million little things—little acts of kindness, little words.

I have a collection of notes, cards, and letters that people have written me over the years that have been extremely encouraging.

One says:

> Just a quick note to encourage you! I really

appreciate your character of kindness and willingness to serve Jesus Christ and everyone else. Keep it up! I'm praying for you. God bless you. P.S. I love you as much as a sister in Christ can!

I feel undeserving, yet inspired and blessed.

Being the encourager can bring enormous rewards as well. I've felt blessed every time I've written someone a cheery note. If I'm feeling blue, it helps just as much to send someone an encouraging letter as receiving one.

Keep the ingredients at hand—a willing spirit, note cards, stationary, envelopes, stamps, and Bible verses that would be appropriate. One friend of mine often includes pressed flowers and leaves whenever she writes to me. It adds a neat little surprise that comes tumbling out.

But don't leave encouragement just for correspondence! As the day passes and the cares of the hour oppress you, give those you pass a smile. Be liberal with words of praise and motivation. You won't regret it.

Be the blessing you are supposed to be—TODAY. "You can do it!"

She Came!

READ: Isaiah 35

It was going to be a depressing weekend for my sister and me. Just a week before, she and her boyfriend had broken their friendship. Now, the approaching weekend, without her usual date, was a reminder of what had been. She felt as if someone had died, and I was gloomy. Vaguely, we anticipated visitors from our church in Pennsylvania several hours away. Even if it were only married couples and children coming, it would at least give us something else to think about.

Saturday afternoon arrived. A little before five, the gray van rolled into our driveway and parked beside the house. And after the door was flung open, who should jump out but one of the girls from our youth group!

She came! The instant I saw her I just knew she cared. Even before she said anything I knew she was there praying for and supporting us.

She came! She skipped the Bike Hike planned for the youth on Saturday, and missed the singing on Sunday evening, just for our sakes.

She came! Together we talked. We talked about how my sister felt and about how he (who had been the boyfriend) must have felt. We cried when we discussed the hurts and the broken dreams. As we talked, our hearts were lightened. Then we talked about what the future might hold, of how God could transform this into something beautiful. We smiled again. In fact, before the weekend ended, we laughed together.

Was she armed with good advice? I don't remember. Little of what she said made an impression on me. But I know that she listened to all that we wanted to talk about. And she came!

Lord, what hurting person is there in my life? Whom do You want me to reach out to today? Whom can I help? So often I falter, not knowing the right words. But Lord, You've reminded me that words may not be the important thing. Sometimes I can show the most support by just being there to share the hurt.

A Spike Needs a Set

READ: Genesis 2:18-25

his world needs men. Men preach the Gospel. Fathers lead godly homes. Businessmen honor God with their money. Men are the leaders. But what can a woman do?

Volleyball games present a similar situation. The fellows make the points. They save the ball when we girls miss it, "dig" when it comes in low, and spike it. How can a girl help in volleyball?

I recently overheard a conversation during a volleyball game. After the ball bounced to my friend, she sent it arching toward the next fellow, setting it for him. He spiked it into the other court, gaining a point for our team. When my friend complimented him, he told her something important. He said this: "You can't spike them like that unless someone first sets them for you."

Ahhh! That is the answer. God didn't create women to lead the world, but to be helpers to the men who can lead it.

Our dads lead our homes. Our brothers stand up in church to lead songs or present topics. The men make important church and business decisions.

However, we still have a role. God created women to set the ball for the men. He wants us to have a character that will inspire the men around us. He wants us to encourage them and support them in prayer.

Do women fill a cavity in men's lives? Yes, because a good spike needs a good set! Will we meet the challenge?

Soul Windows

(Thoughts While Riding a Bus in Guatemala)

READ: John 8:1-11

This sunset could fill a thousand poems,
but not one of them
would do justice to volcanoes
silhouetted with gold and pink.
I barely notice the bus windows,
cracked and darkened,
because, looking beyond them—
I find the sunset.
The pink and gold fades
into black and gray;
yet even in the darkness
the beauty
lingers.
Suddenly, it shatters.
A man boards the bus.
I shudder inside as he staggers
down the aisle, past me.
I see no beauty in this
smelly, greasy-haired person.
I look out the window, and see
nothing but poverty and dirt.
Then, I remember that God
was looking into a window,
cracked and darkened,
when He found—
me.

Lord, help me to see the beauty in each person I meet today,

   the beauty of what they would be like if You found them.

Thank You, too, for seeing the potential in me
   When I was still a sinner.

Lessons From a Tree Hugger

READ: Matthew 28:18-20

Environmental activists, pushed to the extreme by their concern for flora and fauna, have been known to do strange things. But none so strange as Julia Hill who is, quite literally, a tree hugger.

For a full year (and possibly more), this activist has perched in the branches of a northern California redwood. While the magazine update did not allude to Hill's mental state, it did say that she was up there to protest the logging of the redwoods. Through her protests, one lumber company's license was suspended, but Hill still believes that the trees in the forest are in danger. She has no plans to come down.

I found the story a bit hard to believe, but there was a picture of Julia Hill crouched on a branch, her arms wrapped around the trunk. She looked normal enough, so determined in her conviction that she was helping the trees. She had beliefs, and she acted upon them.

A lesson for you and me? Yes.

No, I'm not suggesting that we pattern our lives after her. But I am suggesting that we pursue our loyalties to the kingdom of God.

Really, how much are we doing for Him? Would we be willing (like Julia Hill) to spend a year, not in a tree but maybe other strange places, in the service of the Lord? Would we be willing, in spite of ridicule, to do things for God that might look strange to the rest of the world?

"Dear God, I want to be ready and willing to be an activist for Your kingdom. Help me to be bold in sharing Jesus and unashamedly living a holy life. I want to serve You until You call me home."

Open My Door

READS: Revelation 3:7-13

On that lovely spring day, the birds were singing as I walked along the dirt road up the mountain. Happy and carefree, I drank in the beauty of nature. How delicious it was to be alive just then!

I noticed a crumbling, boarded-up shack beside the road. An elderly lady shuffled out the door, and began sweeping her tiny walk with a bit of a broom. An old coat was pulled over her plump figure, and gray curls peeped underneath her cap.

Glancing up, the lady spied me walking toward her. "BANG!" The door slammed behind her hastily retreating figure. At any rate, she didn't appreciate my presence!

Recovering from my surprise, I thought, *How sad! I can't even imagine how isolated this poor lady is!* I probably would have greeted her as I passed, or maybe even talked to her. Before I had a chance, she made it plain that she didn't want any interference!

I had to think, that sometimes I am like that old lady. When I know that someone has needs that I can identify with, I shut myself up because I don't want to be exposed. Rather than reaching out to my community, I hide in my little shack because I don't feel like taking the time or effort needed to show someone I care. And I don't even realize the joy I am depriving myself of.

I pray that God would speak to that lady, and soften her cold heart. I also pray that God would touch *my* heart. I want to always keep my door wide open to the needs of others.

187

Lilies and Lives

READ: James 4:14; Psalm 90:1-12

Lily peeked out through her opening petals. "Oh, what a beautiful world!" she exclaimed. She stretched to get a better view of the sunrise. Looking around, she saw the rest of the lilies that had also opened that morning.

"Yes, it is pretty," another lily said. "I wonder what the mistress will say about us. I hope she comes soon."

Lily turned again toward the sun. The warmth of its rays on her petals filled her with pleasure.

A rose spoke up. Looking at the young flower, she said, "Lily, enjoy this day because…"

The sound of footsteps interrupted her. Lily saw an approaching lady…the mistress! She bent over and looked at the new rose buds. She caressed their soft petals. Touching all her flowers, she went on.

Lily raised herself higher, so the mistress would be sure to see her.

"My day lilies!" the mistress exclaimed lovingly. "My beautiful, beautiful day lilies!" She touched Lily's soft, orange petals, exclaiming over her beauty. Oh, how Lily loved that touch!

The mistress spoke again, this time with pain in her voice. "My day lilies, enjoy your life as much as you can, because very soon it will be over. Day lilies live only from sunrise to sunset. But, oh, how much joy you bring to me! You make me very happy, especially if you enjoy yourselves in your short life."

After the mistress left, Lily felt like crying. She hadn't known she'd die so soon. She had just unfolded that morning!

Her mistress' words came back to her. *Joy to my mistress! Yes, that's what she said! My short life can bring a little ray of happiness to others, just like the sunrays give to me. So that's what I was made for— to bring color to the world for one day.*

Lily looked up. "Sun," she whispered softly. "Just as you bring me joy for a day, I will pass it on in my one-day life. I will radiate happiness in this garden, even if it's only for one short day."

*   *   *   *

Just as Lily, I too, might have a short life. I know that my Master, Jesus Christ, loves me. His caring touch means more than I can say. He loves me much, much more than the mistress loved Lily. His love makes life worth living.

I want to radiate the joy and happiness that Jesus has given me. That way, my short life will have served its purpose.

Chapter 13

Where Will You Be?

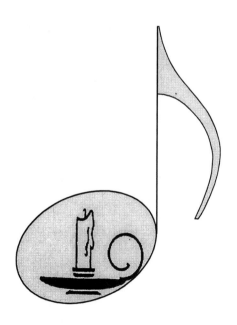

In a Hundred Years

READ: Revelation 21:3-7

In a hundred years, it will not matter that your sister broke your heirloom doll.

In a hundred years, it will not matter that your brother tore the cover on the book you got for your birthday.

In a hundred years it will not matter that your mother will not let you make your new dress in the latest style.

In a hundred years, it will not matter that your father will not let you ride home from a youth gathering with a boy you like.

In a hundred years, these little family conflicts will not matter. In fact, will they matter in fifty years? Twenty? Ten? Next year? Tomorrow? Many of your small, everyday conflicts are of no importance even in the next hour.

What *does* matter is your response to these frictions and your attitudes to the people involved. Those *will* matter in a hundred years, because they will effect your eternal destination.

The birthplace of your attitudes and responses is in the mind. Control there, when the root of bitterness is small, could determine who you become and where you go.

"Watch your thoughts; they become words.

Watch your words; they become actions.

Watch your actions; they become habits.

Watch your habits; they become character.

Watch your character; it becomes destiny."

—Anonymous

192

An Unlit Candle

READ: Psalm 119:89-112

One night I went to turn off our generator, and decided to grab an extra candle while I was downstairs. I was too lazy to light it. I figured I should know the way to my bedroom well enough to get there in the dark. But when I crashed into a piece of furniture on the way, I thought, "How foolish it would look to see me fumbling in the dark holding an unlit candle!"

What is guiding me through life? Am I stumbling in the darkness of this world, figuring I can make it on my own? Or, am I relying on God and His Word to give me direction?

I've been raised in a Christian family. I've heard Bible stories all of my life. I've gone to church regularly and have heard inspiring sermons. I've gone to Bible school. I know what is expected of me, and I think I know the right way to go. But that isn't enough. I also need to take time daily to study the Word, to find out what God is saying to me personally. I need to meditate on His Word—and obey it too!

If I use the Word to light my pathway towards heaven, there will be no doubt of my destination.

Empty Bags

READS: *Hebrews 6:1-12*

"Victoria, why are those plastic bags hanging on that tree by the lane?" I asked curiously. On the lower branches of the tree hung two empty bags, and I couldn't imagine how they got there.

"Oh that," Victoria replied. "Lovelle and I were on our way to the creek to gather meadow tea. But then Daddy came home, so we just hung our bags on the tree."

I smiled to myself at the incident. When Dad comes home from work, all else is forgotten. That explained the mysterious bags hanging on the tree.

Actually, a lot of people leave their bags hanging on the trees. Somehow, we just don't get around to filling our bags. We have so many other interesting and pressing things to do. Most of us would admit that often we are too lazy, and make excuses because we'd rather not take the time or effort required to fill our bags. Of course, *someday...*

But "someday" may never come. When our Father returns, will He find the work undone? Will your tea bag still be hanging on the tree?

Reflections on Death

READ: Romans 6

Most of us do not like to think about death. Death seems to be a brutal enemy that thrusts us into the abyss of eternity. Death is chillingly final. It separates families, breaks hearts, and brings us to judgment. Death is cruel.

We try to reassure ourselves that death is only for others outside of our family, or the elderly. Surely death would not rob us while we are yet so young and have so much potential. Death seems too terrible to crush a young person.

Yet, we cannot deny that death is no respecter of persons. My sweet, loving cousin was only seven years old when she died of a brain aneurysm. My friend was thrown off a horse and hovered at the threshold of death. A fourteen year old was killed in a farm accident. A schoolteacher died suddenly.

In light of death, the latest fads, fancy houses (or bedrooms), and superficial amusements lose importance. Peer pressure and popularity vanish. Our selfishness looms in front of us, and we suddenly see that our family, our relationships, our obedience to authority, and our walk with God are crucial. Our wasted time, our disrespect, and our pride will mock us in the face of death.

Besides the physical death, there is a second death. We have the choice for this death. It is either death to sin or death in hell. Our burden of sin drags us down the chasm to hell, and we have no power to stop. Many flail helplessly, trying to grasp some tiny thread of moral goodness, scientific logic, or a religious front to keep them from falling, but it is no use. No human power can keep anyone from going to hell.

In that chasm of sin and death, there is a shining way.

Illuminated in the way stands the old rugged cross. When, we, as weary sinners, crucify self on the cross, the burden of sin rolls off. We are enabled to climb the difficult, but passable, way out of the chasm. We are admitted to the glorious City, and God Himself takes us into His presence.

When sin is nailed to the cross, death is not death. It is life!

The Best Is Yet to Be

READ: Isaiah 58:8-12

Sometimes I wonder what is best
    in the way that I should go.
Sometimes I really struggle
    because I really want to know.
I want God's will, but it is hard
    to know what's right for me,
But 'midst these thoughts I firmly feel
    the best is yet to be.

"I know the plans I have for you, "
    I hear my Savior say;
"Plans to prosper, not to harm you,
    if you willingly obey.

Listen closely, I will tell you,
 look around and you will see,
Things look dark for now, I know,
 but *the best is yet to be.*"

This will, this plan, God has for me
 may not be what I think.
I can struggle, I can fight it,
 from my duty I may shrink.
But no peace will be my pillow,
 and my dreams will not be free
'Til I yield my own desirings,
 'cause *the best is yet to be.*

There is beauty in this trusting,
 my life with riches He can fill.
I know the best, God's best for me,
 is being in His perfect will.
God's will is the best for now,
 but there's a *better* best for me—
There's a heaven in my vision,
 and *the best is yet to be.*

Feeling at Home

READ: John 14:1-4

Awkward situations are not things I enjoy. I'm sure no one likes them, but sometimes it seems like I land in them more than others do. I've often wished that I could feel totally at ease wherever I go, walk with a natural grace, always say appropriate things, and smile at all the right times.

I have thought that if I'd just be a little different, or even if my friends were a little different, I would be carefree and happy.

Then I read this saying: "No worse fate can befall a person than to be completely at home in this life."

There is a lot of truth in that saying. If I felt completely at home in this life, I wouldn't have a reason to look forward to heaven.

I'm trying to look at the discomforts and imperfections in my life as blessings in disguise. Why? These things remind me that earth is temporary.

Once I'm in heaven, I will feel completely at home—forever!

Another Good Thing About Heaven

READ: Isaiah 65:17-25

Sometimes I'm not extremely eager to reach heaven. I feel as if I've got a lot of things left to experience on earth. But God, in His wisdom, has many ways of reminding me that life on earth is not as nice as I sometimes think it is.

At the youth fellowships meetings the year after I went to Bible School, I knew an overwhelming number of people. When I came home, I kept thinking of people that I'd never even said "hi" to. I felt unfinished and regretful. Even when I decided that there was no way I could have talked with everyone I knew, I still didn't feel much better.

Finally I realized that there is only one place where relationships can be perfect. I think that if I would get a glimpse of the perfection of heaven, I'd be more eager to go there. Perfect relationships, complete harmony with everyone I'm with, always knowing what to say next—that sounds terrific, doesn't it?

I want to be able to say honestly, "My soul longeth, yea, even fainteth for the courts of the Lord: my heart and my flesh crieth out for the living God" (Psalm 84:20). There are so many good—and perfect—things about heaven!

If There is Not Harmony in Your Heart
and you do not know Jesus

Perhaps you feel a keen disconnection with the heartbeat of this book. Although we have written of suffering, temptations, difficult experiences, and human failings, all of us have experienced on a deep, personal level the work of Jesus. In every circumstance, Jesus can untangle the knots in our lives and bring harmony to our hearts. Maybe you don't experience this. What should you do?

First, you must realize that you have utterly failed to attain to God's standards, and even your good works are, to Him, as filthy rags. As a wretched sinner, you are cut off from God and cannot have fellowship with Him. Sin (disobedience to God's commandments) not only controls you, it condemns you.

Your own good works cannot justify you; if you try to "balance" your bad deeds with good deeds, you will discover that a balance is impossible because of your sinful nature. Therefore, you must admit that you are totally helpless and cannot justify or save yourself.

God owes humanity nothing. He does not *need* you. Amazingly, God, in His infinite, unfathomable love, *desires* an intimate relationship with you. He longs to cleanse you from your sin. Jesus Christ is the only remedy, the only one who can open the lines of communication between you and God.

Secondly, confess your sins. Satan has strongholds on your life that can only be broken by confessing your sinful thoughts, words, and acts to God. Confess specifically and in detail, hold nothing back from God so that He can break those strongholds, heal and cleanse your heart.

Following confession, repent, and turn away from sin.

Grieve your sinful past, the hurt you have caused yourself and others, and your separation from God. Repentance should become a way of life for you, a constant turning from sin.

When you realize that you are totally incapable of repaying the debt you owe, and you confess and repent of your sinful life, you are ready to believe in the atonement of Jesus' blood to cleanse you from sin. He died for *you*, bore your sins to Calvary where he gave his life on the cross for you. Not only did Jesus die, He arose from the grave to give new life to all who believe on Him!

As you approach God by faith, and believe that Jesus' blood is sufficient to erase your sins, God will declare you free from guilt and acceptable to Him! Because of God's *grace* (God's favor to you and His strength within you), sin no longer controls you. God fills your spirit with His Spirit, and your spirit becomes sanctified, new, holy. You are a saint instead of a sinner!

Entering into your life, the Holy Spirit will convict you of sinful patterns and habits that you need to break. By following the Spirit, living in total submission and obedience to Him, your heart will become cleansed and purified. This refining of the heart is a gradual process, and you will still make mistakes, but God's grace covers your shortcomings so long as you are still *wholeheartedly* following the Spirit. Spiritual fruits and gifts will develop in your life, to help you minister to the lost and needy souls around you.

While grace abundantly covers your human mistakes, if you reject the Holy Spirit's leading or do things contrary to God's will, you will start down the path to spiritual death. Trusting and obeying the Holy Spirit is crucial to your Christian life.

After you believe on Jesus and become a Christian, you will need to be baptized. Join a Biblically sound church where Christ is preached and the Bible is the final authority.

A few important pointers:

-Read your Bible every day. The answer to any question can be found in the Word of God. God will reveal His plan for your life, convict you of sin, refresh, and comfort you.

-Talk to God in prayer every day. He is interested in even the smallest details of your life, nothing is too great or small for God! He will share His love and guidance with you as you develop an intimate relationship with Him.

-Worship God and fellowship with other baptized Christians in a church that is based on the Bible. Get involved with your church and fellow Christians.

-Tell others about salvation. Make an effort to spread the news of Jesus, and His unsurpassable love. Share what Jesus has done for you!

As a Christian, your struggles will not be stumbling blocks, but stepping stones to draw you closer to God! A daughter of God, freed from the bondage of sin and fear, you can rejoice and enjoy your fellowship with God. You will encounter difficulties, your faith will be severely tried, but when you are on God's side, you have nothing to fear. Remain faithful, Heaven awaits for you if you persevere!

Only Jesus can touch the discordant keys of our poor human ways, and change them to peaceful harmonies that show forth His praise. Only Jesus can bring harmony to your heart. He will be your strength and song!

If you do not have the harmony that comes from knowing Jesus, pray to Him asking Him to change your life!

Dear Lord, I realize that I am a sinner, lost and cut off from You. I confess _____(list sins specifically) *and I ask You to break Satan's strongholds on my life. I repent of my sinful life, and I long for You to make me righteous and pure. I believe that Jesus died for me and arose from the grave. I believe that his blood can cleanse me from sin. Fill me with your Spirit and help me live a Christian life. In Jesus' name I pray, Amen.*

What Does the Bible Say About Sin?

1. Our sinfulness:

"Wherefore as by one man sin entered into the world, and death by sin; and so death passed upon all men, for that all have sinned." Romans 5:12

"All have sinned and come short of the glory of God." Romans 3:23

"The wages of sin is death, but the gift of God is eternal life through Jesus Christ our Lord." Romans 6:23

2. Confession of sin:

"He that covereth his sins shall not prosper, but whoso confesseth and forsaketh them shall have mercy." Proverbs 28:13

"If we confess our sins, he is faithful and just to forgive us our sins, and to cleanse us from all unrighteousness." I John 1:9

3. Repentance of sin:

"Thine own wickedness shall correct thee, and thy backslidings shall reprove thee: know therefore and see that it is an evil thing and bitter, that thou hast forsaken the Lord thy God, and that my fear is not in thee, saith the Lord God of hosts." Jeremiah 2:19

"If my people, which are called by my name, shall humble themselves, and pray, and seek my face, and turn from their wicked ways; then will I hear from heaven and will forgive their sin, and will heal their land." 2 Chronicles 7:14

"I tell you, Nay: but, except ye repent, ye shall all likewise perish." Luke 13:5

4. Salvation from sin:

"For God so loved the world, that he gave his only begotten Son, that whosoever believeth in him should not perish, but have everlasting life." John 3:16

"Neither is there salvation in any other, for there is no other name under heaven given among men whereby ye must be saved." Acts 4:12

"If thou shalt confess with thy mouth the Lord Jesus, and shalt believe in thine heart that God hath raised him from the dead, thou shalt be saved. For with the heart man believeth unto righteousness; and with the mouth confession is made unto salvation." Romans 10:9,10

5. Living above sin:

"Therefore, if any man be in Christ, he is a new creature: old things are passed away; behold, all things are become new." 2 Corinthians 5:17

"But as many as received him, to them gave he power to become the sons of God, even to them that believe on his name." John 1:12

"Come unto me, all ye that labour and are heavy laden, and I will give you rest. Take my yoke upon you, and learn of me; for I am meek and lowly in heart: and ye shall find rest unto your souls. For my yoke is easy and my burden is light." Matthew 11:28-30

BIOGRAPHICAL SKETCHES
at the time of writing
Each devotional is identified by the writer's key signature.

Elaine Berry was born in the Shenandoah Valley of Virginia. When she was fifteen, her family moved to Seymour, Missouri. Trips to Puerto Rico, Mexico, Belize, Guatemala, El Salvador, and Honduras have given her a love for Latin America and its people. She is currently teaching school in Estacada, Oregon.

Jane Eberly lives on a ranch in south central Montana. A move from Minnesota, where her family had lived ten years, was a difficult time for Jane, but it taught her more trust in God. In 2000, she went to Mexico with a group of young people to work at various missions. She plans to return to Chihuaha, Mexico, to help a missionary family there.

Maryann Eby's family moved from Hagerstown, Maryland, to Guatemala in 1986. Living there has been a good experience for her as she has learned to relate to different people and situations. She and her family are serving in Guatemala City under Mennonite Air Missions. Several youth Bible Institutes held in Guatemala have been an encouragement to her.

Karen Glick has lived in El Salvador all her life, close to Candelaria de la Frontera. In 1993, her father was kidnapped on a mountain where he had gone to hold services. Prayers for his release were answered, and this has helped Karen to have a deeper appreciation for her father and more trust in God. At the time of this writing, she is teaching school in El Salvador.

Rachel Graybill Musser lived most of her life in Pennsylvania. A chorus tour to Haiti with Sharon Mennonite Singers, and a month spent in Romania at Christian Aid Ministries' orphanage, helped to prepare her for a time of service in Guatemala. She was a nurse at the Good Samaritan Clinic in El Chal for three years. She moved back to Pennsylvania in 1999 and married Steve Musser.

Heather Martin grew up on a hog farm in New York state. Her family is anticipating a move to Pennsylvania soon. In 1998, she went on a twelve-day trip to Belize, and left part of her heart there. She is looking forward to a year of teaching school in Blue Creek, Belize, under Caribbean Light and Truth.

Rosina Miller was born in Iowa and lived there for eleven years of her life. In 1993, her family moved to Honey Grove, Pennsylvania. She enjoyed a month spent in Romania in 1998. Rosina was born moderately deaf, and after additional losses received a cochlear implant to restore her hearing. She enjoys working on the family produce farm, private tutoring, substitute teaching, and part-time typesetting for Green Pasture Press.

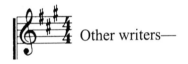 Sherilyn Troyer is from Plain City, Ohio. She attended Calvary Bible School for six weeks in 1997 and three weeks in 1998. She is an assistant secretary for Friesen Fabricating & Equipment Company, and also works as a veterinary assistant at the Plain City Animal Hospital. She has been helping with weekly children's classes at an inner-city mission.

Other writers—

Kathryn Glick (Isabella Bank, Belize)
Do I Have Time?
Quadratic Equations
Quality Christians

Rachel Kuepfer (Kisumu, Kenya)
Does God Hear?
The Fires of God

Susana Martin (El Novillero, Guatemala)
If You Love Something